PLAYING JULIET/ CASTING OTHELLO

Two Plays
by
CALEEN SINNETTE JENNINGS

Playing Juliet
and
Casting Othello

Dramatic Publishing
Woodstock, Illinois • London, England • Melbourne, Australia

*** NOTICE ***

The amateur and stock acting rights to this work are controlled exclusively by THE DRAMATIC PUBLISHING COMPANY without whose permission in writing no performance of it may be given. Royalty fees are given in our current catalog and are subject to change without notice. Royalty must be paid every time a play is performed whether or not it is presented for profit and whether or not admission is charged. A play is performed any time it is acted before an audience. All inquiries concerning amateur and stock rights should be addressed to:

DRAMATIC PUBLISHING
P. O. Box 129, Woodstock, Illinois 60098

COPYRIGHT LAW GIVES THE AUTHOR OR THE AUTHOR'S AGENT *THE EXCLUSIVE RIGHT TO MAKE COPIES.* This law provides authors with a fair return for their creative efforts. Authors earn their living from the royalties they receive from book sales and from the performance of their work. Conscientious observance of copyright law is not only ethical, it encourages authors to continue their creative work. This work is fully protected by copyright. No alterations, deletions or substitutions may be made in the work without the prior written consent of the publisher. No part of this work may be reproduced or transmitted in any form or by any means, electronic or mechanical, including photocopy, recording, videotape, film, or any information storage and retrieval system, without permission in writing from the publisher. It may not be performed either by professionals or amateurs without payment of royalty. All rights, including but not limited to the professional, motion picture, radio, television, videotape, foreign language, tabloid, recitation, lecturing, publication, and reading are reserved.

For performance of any songs and recordings mentioned in this play which are in copyright, the permission of the copyright owners must be obtained or other songs and recordings in the public domain substituted.

©MCMXCIX by
CALEEN SINNETTE JENNINGS

Printed in the United States of America
All Rights Reserved
(PLAYING JULIET/CASTING OTHELLO)

ISBN 0-87129-924-0

IMPORTANT BILLING AND CREDIT REQUIREMENTS

All producers of the play *must* give credit to the author(s) of the play in all programs distributed in connection with performances of the play and in all instances in which the title of the play appears for purposes of advertising, publicizing or otherwise exploiting the play and/or a production. The name of the author(s) *must* also appear on a separate line, on which no other name appears, immediately following the title, and *must* appear in size of type not less than fifty percent the size of the title type. Biographical information on the author(s), if included in this book, may be used on all programs. *On all programs this notice must appear:*

"Produced by special arrangement with
THE DRAMATIC PUBLISHING COMPANY of Woodstock, Illinois"

For my family:
Carl, Robeson, DuBois, Calvin,
Elinor, Dee, Jerry, Lucas, and Norma.

PLAYING JULIET/CASTING OTHELLO

Two One-act Plays
For a biracial cast of 6
(3 women and 3 men, all are 25-45 years old)

Contents

Acknowledgments................................. 6

Playing Juliet 7
Casting Othello.................................. 54

Casting Othello was first performed in showcase in 1996 at The Source Theatre Company's 16th annual Washington Summer Theatre Festival, Pat Murphy Sheehy, Artistic Director; Garland Scott, Associate Producer; and Keith Parker, Literary Manager. It was directed by Lisa Rose Middleton.

Playing Juliet/Casting Othello was co-produced in 1998 by the Folger Shakespeare Library (Werner Gundesheimer, Executive Director; and Janet Alexander Griffin, Director of Museum and Public Programs) and The Source Theatre Company (Joe Banno, Artistic Director; DeAnna Duncan, Managing Director; and Keith Parker, Literary Manager). It was directed by Lisa Rose Middleton. The cast was as follows:

Georgia	KILA D. BURTON
Jimmy	SCOTT LEONARD FORTUNE
Wendy	SUSAN LINSKEY
Dave	STEVE LEBENS
Chris	JEFF MANDON
Lorraine	RACHEL D. SPAGHT

Thanks

Heartfelt thanks to all who made the published script and the first production of this play possible: Gayle Sergel, Lisa Rose Middleton, Scott Leonard Fortune and the rest of the wonderful cast and crew, Bill and Louisa Newlin, Peggy O'Brien and Michael Tolaydo, Patricia Thornton, Janet Griffin, Joe Banno, DeAnna Duncan, Pat Murphy Sheehy, Keith Parker, and Gail Humphries.

PLAYING JULIET

CHARACTERS

LORRAINE (plays Juliet's nurse) .... Light-skinned African American.

CHRIS (plays Romeo) .... White.

WENDY .... White, director of the production.

GEORGIA (plays Juliet).. Dark-skinned African American.

DAVID (plays Capulet, is also production stage manager) White, seasoned actor, slightly older than the others.

JIMMY .... African American, Georgia's boyfriend. Smart, working class, a non-actor.

TIME:
The present.

SETTING:
New Vistas, a tiny theatre outside of a major U.S. city.

PLAYING JULIET

SCENE: *New Vistas Theatre. The group is a small step up from community theatre, having received some funding and notoriety. They operate with no budget, have very little time, but have high ideals. All but CHRIS have job jobs! A clutter of half-finished scenery. Work lights, bare walls. Rehearsal cubes, flats, props, pieces half-constructed are scattered about. Perhaps the upstage wall is the exposed brick wall of the building.*

AT RISE: *Lights up on LORRAINE and CHRIS doing the famous balcony scene from Shakespeare's* Romeo and Juliet. *WENDY watches from the house. DAVE is on book.*

LORRAINE as JULIET.
>Hist! Romeo, hist! O! for a falconer's voice,
>To lure this tassel-gentle back again.
>Bondage is hoarse, and may not speak aloud,
>Else would I tear the cave where Echo lies,
>And make her airy tongue more hoarse than mine,
>With repetition of my Romeo's name.

CHRIS as ROMEO.
>It is my soul that calls upon my name:
>How silver-sweet sound lovers' tongues by night,
>Like softest music to attending ears!

JULIET.
> Romeo!

ROMEO.
> My dear!

JULIET.
> At what o'clock tomorrow
> Shall I send to thee?

ROMEO.
> At the hour of nine.

JULIET.
> I will not fail; 'tis twenty years till then.
> I have forgot why I did call thee back.

ROMEO.
> Let me stand here till thou remember it. *(They kiss.)*

JULIET.
> I shall forget, to have thee still stand there,
> Remembering how I love thy company *(They kiss.)*

ROMEO.
> And I'll stay, to have thee still forget,
> Forgetting any other home but this. *(They kiss.)*

(Unseen by all, GEORGIA enters and watches the rest of the scene.)

JULIET.
>Tis almost morning; I would have thee gone;
>And yet no further than a wanton's bird,
>Who lets it hop a little from her hand,
>Like a poor prisoner in his twisted gyves,
>And with a silk thread plucks it back again,
>So loving jealous of his liberty.

ROMEO.
>I would I were thy bird

JULIET.
>Sweet, so would I
>Yet I should kill thee with much cherishing. *(They kiss.)*

GEORGIA *(interrupting)*. I'm here. *(Everyone is startled.)*
WENDY. Georgia. I didn't see you.
LORRAINE. Hey, G.
GEORGIA. All that kissing wasn't in there.
WENDY. No, but it works.
CHRIS *(sarcastically)*. Nice of you to drop in.
DAVE. Are we doing fines?
GEORGIA. I had to wait for a bus.
CHRIS *(under his breath)*. For two hours?
WENDY. Waive the fine.
CHRIS. You fined me last week and I was only twenty minutes late.
GEORGIA. I guess that made a real dent in your wallet, huh.
DAVE. Let's get going. We're behind.
WENDY. Lorraine was helping Chris run lines while we waited for you. Thanks, Lorraine, you were great.

GEORGIA. She sure was. *(Taking off her coat.)* But I'm not doing all that kissing.
CHRIS *(under his breath)*. Just doing the lines would be an improvement. *(LORRAINE hits CHRIS lightly.)*
GEORGIA *(to LORRAINE)*. What did he say?
WENDY. Never mind. Let's do a warmup.
GEORGIA. Let's not and say we did.
WENDY. I think it's important that we take a minute to...
GEORGIA. My stomach is killing me.
LORRAINE. You really brighten up a rehearsal, G.
GEORGIA. Anybody ask you?
WENDY *(with false cheer)*. Well then, let's just jump into the scene. Don't we love acting?
DAVE. Act II, Scene 2, from Juliet, "Hist, hist."

(LORRAINE moves offstage. GEORGIA takes her place. The scene begins again. All the sensuality and longing we saw between CHRIS and LORRAINE in the scene is now non-existent. GEORGIA plays it formally, almost with an attitude.)

GEORGIA as JULIET.
    Hist! Romeo, hist! O! for a falconer's voice,
    To lure this tassel-gentle back again.
    Bondage is hoarse, and may not speak aloud,
    Else would I tear the cave where Echo lies,
    And make her airy tongue more hoarse than mine,
    With repetition of my Romeo's name.

CHRIS as ROMEO.
    It is my soul that calls upon my name:

How silver-sweet sound lovers' tongues by night,
Like softest music to attending ears!

JULIET.
    Romeo!

ROMEO.
    My dear!

JULIET.
    At what o'clock tomorrow
    Shall I send to thee?

ROMEO.
    At the hour of nine.

JULIET.
    I will not fail; 'tis twenty years till then.
    I have forgot why I did call thee back.

ROMEO.
    Let me stand here till thou remember it.
    (CHRIS tries to kiss GEORGIA, but she turns her head.)

JULIET.
    I shall forget, to have thee still stand there,
    Remembering how I love thy company
    (CHRIS tries to kiss GEORGIA again, but she moves away.)

ROMEO.
    And I'll stay, to have thee still forget,
    Forgetting any other home but this.

JULIET.
> 'Tis almost morning; I would have thee gone;
> And yet no further than a wanton's bird,
> Who lets it hop a little from her hand,
> Like a poor prisoner in his twisted gyves,
> And with a silk thread plucks it back again,
> So loving jealous of his liberty.

ROMEO.
> I would I were thy bird

JULIET.
> Sweet, so would I
> Yet I should kill thee with much cherishing.

(CHRIS tries to kiss GEORGIA, but she puts up her hand.)

WENDY. Okay, hold it!
GEORGIA *(defensively)*. I know my lines.
CHRIS. What is this, "Taming of the Shrew"?
WENDY. Your acting choices are somewhat unusual.
GEORGIA. And you like Lorraine's better?
DAVE. We need warmth, passion, longing.
WENDY *(hushing DAVE)*. Thank you, Dave. *(To GEORGIA and CHRIS.)* You guys are supposed to be hot for each other.
GEORGIA. My stomach's upset.
CHRIS. I've been known to have that effect.
GEORGIA. I gotta use the bathroom.
WENDY. Let's take five and we'll do it again.

(GEORGIA exits to a bathroom. DAVE approaches WENDY with his "To Do" list.)

DAVE. The printer's bringing the programs for a final proof. Theresa wants to know if we can afford to rent those little hats and whether you want white lace on the court ladies.

WENDY. Don't give my actors notes, okay?

DAVE. I was just...

WENDY. I know, but don't.

DAVE. Sorry.

LORRAINE. Anybody want anything? I'm going out.

DAVE. I'd kill for a light, extra sugar. You sure you don't mind?

LORRAINE. Nah.

DAVE *(handing LORRAINE money)*. And bring Wendy a regular.

WENDY *(fishing for money in her purse)*. I've got it, Dave.

DAVE. I already gave it to her.

WENDY. No, I've got it.

DAVE. I *can* spare a buck.

WENDY. I don't like to owe anyone. *(Hands money to DAVE.)* Here.

DAVE. Jeez.

WENDY. I'm gonna call Theresa. Start them on the scene as soon as Georgia's out of the can. Just run the lines. And don't direct! *(She exits talking to herself.)*

DAVE. All right. All right. *(He exits backstage.)*

LORRAINE. What do you want?

CHRIS. What I can't have.

LORRAINE. Something that's good for you.

CHRIS. Not interested.

LORRAINE. You're getting better.

CHRIS. I shoulda stayed in L.A.

LORRAINE. And fried up the little bit of brains you had left? You looked like a dog when you got here. Now you're healthy and your work's good.

CHRIS. Yeah, right. I make Juliet nauseous.

LORRAINE. Stop being so down on yourself.

CHRIS. I haven't done Shakespeare since college. My audition was awful. You think Wendy would have cast me if my daddy wasn't on New Vistas' board?

LORRAINE. No.

CHRIS. Thanks.

LORRAINE. Why ask if you don't want the truth?

CHRIS. In L.A. we always taped. We never used live audiences. Looking at all those seats gives me the chills. I bet Dad'll sit right there.

LORRAINE. So what.

CHRIS. Am I any good?

LORRAINE. For an ex-cokehead, soap star, has-been from L.A., you're pretty good.

CHRIS. Was that supposed to be a compliment?

LORRAINE. Lucky to get that!

CHRIS. You gonna go out with me?

LORRAINE. What you smoking?

CHRIS. Woman, you're rough.

LORRAINE *(quoting Benvolio).* "If love be rough with you, be rough with love"

CHRIS. You saying you love me?

LORRAINE. In your dreams.

(WENDY approaches from the back of the house.)

WENDY. She out yet?
LORRAINE. Nah. I'm gone.
WENDY. And hurry back. I want to do Juliet/Nurse II-5.
LORRAINE. Okay. *(She exits.)*
CHRIS. I'll go with her.
WENDY. Uh-uh. I need you here.
CHRIS. I need some air.
WENDY. Stick your head out of the door for two minutes.
CHRIS *(running out)*. Hey, Lorraine!

(DAVE enters.)

DAVE. We're two and a half hours behind schedule.
WENDY. I know that. Is Georgia ready?
DAVE. She's throwing up.
WENDY. Great.
DAVE. I left a message for her boyfriend in case she needs to be taken home.
WENDY. He won't come.
DAVE. If she has to go home...
WENDY. I'll put her in a cab.
DAVE *(going down his list)*. Three high schools reserved for the matinee. The Board wants you to stage some scenes for the fund raiser next week.
WENDY. Terrific!
DAVE. Kingsley says the wood's gonna cost more than he thought. He wants you to call him tomorrow. We're quite a bit over budget, and you'd better clear it with...
WENDY. I know, Dave. I know.
DAVE. We're not going to get to any of the fight stuff. Want me to catch Mercutio, Benvolio and the Friar? We'll have to tag them onto tomorrow's schedule.

WENDY. Depends on what happens tonight. Ask me in an hour.

DAVE. You thought about my idea for the chorus?

WENDY. Not really.

DAVE. Since the chorus is the tie to the audience that...

WENDY. I know the function of the chorus.

DAVE. If you staged the tableaux, you could...

WENDY. I'll keep what I've got.

DAVE. You really think Glen Fisher has the power to pull off...

WENDY. What is your problem?

DAVE. I'm just asking.

WENDY. Do me a favor. Leave the artistic decisions to me and prepare for II-2.

DAVE. Sure. Look, the show's going to be fine.

WENDY. I don't need a pep talk, Dave. I really don't.

(CHRIS enters from back of the house.)

CHRIS. She out yet?

WENDY. I'll check on her. You stay here. *(She exits backstage.)*

DAVE *(hands CHRIS several messages and sets up cubes for the balcony scene)*. From your dad.

CHRIS *(reading the slips)*. Only seven this time.

DAVE. He's just worried about you.

CHRIS. He's checking up on me. I feel like a teenager again.

DAVE. Use if for Romeo.

CHRIS. The shrink says this is a test of our new relationship. I know when I think of him sitting front row center, my guts turn to rice pudding. I'm such a wimp. No wonder Lorraine won't give me the time of day. You got any advice?

DAVE. On what?

CHRIS. Love.

DAVE. Ha. Wish I did. Maybe I'd do better myself. Better ask someone else for advice on love. Want to run lines?

CHRIS. No offense, but I'd rather run lines with Juliet for a change.

DAVE. Georgia's really a wonderful actor. She's just got a lot going on in her life right now.

CHRIS. And I don't? This crap is hard enough without her nonsense.

DAVE. Are you referring to the Bard as "this crap"?

CHRIS. I'm sweating bullets, man.

(WENDY enters.)

WENDY. She's coming.

CHRIS. Wendy, this stinks.

WENDY. Just relax, Chris.

CHRIS. I bet she doesn't know her lines for the end of the scene.

WENDY. She'll get it together.

CHRIS. I mean I really like her, but...

(GEORGIA enters.)

GEORGIA. But what?

WENDY. You've got to stop doing that.

GEORGIA. What?

CHRIS. Sneaking up on people.

GEORGIA. You learn a lot that way.

CHRIS. It's not fair.
GEORGIA. Nothing is fair.
WENDY. Dave, we're ready. Top of II-2.
DAVE. Top? They just did the ending?
WENDY. It was terrible. Why am I explaining this to you? Just do what I ask. Actors, are you ready?
DAVE. Places for the top of II-2. Your lines okay for this, Georgia?
GEORGIA. I'm sort of off book, but be there for me.
CHRIS. Sort of?
GEORGIA. Yes. Sort of. I know most of it.
CHRIS. Great.
GEORGIA. Shut up.
WENDY. Hey, hey!
GEORGIA. Tell him to lay off.
CHRIS. We open in twelve days, Georgia, my love.
GEORGIA. I'll be ready.
CHRIS. And we're supposed to take your word on that?
WENDY *(exasperated)*. How much of the scene do you know, Georgia?
GEORGIA. Most of it.
WENDY *(to CHRIS and DAVE)*. Excuse us a sec. *(She takes GEORGIA to one side.)*
CHRIS *(to DAVE)*. You believe this?
DAVE. Take it easy. Run lines with me. *(CHRIS sits close to DAVE, running lines in a murmur.)*
WENDY. I've never seen you like this. Your work is flaky and you look awful.
GEORGIA. Thanks.
WENDY. You're late to rehearsal with an attitude a mile thick. This isn't like you.

GEORGIA. I'm sorry. I'm truly sorry. I'll know my lines by tomorrow.

WENDY. You said that last week. *(Slight pause.)* What's up with Jimmy?

GEORGIA. Get off my case, Wendy.

WENDY. I haven't even started. My butt is swinging in the breeze here, G.

GEORGIA. And mine isn't?

WENDY. How can I help you?

GEORGIA. Keep your smart-mouth Romeo on a leash.

WENDY. What do you want me to say to him? You know whose kid he is. Besides, *he's* off book. He's the least of my worries. My set is a heap. We're over budget. Dave's breathing down my neck and my Juliet's on Mars.

GEORGIA. I've got a lot on my mind.

WENDY. As your friend, I'm saying, I know and I'm sorry. As your director, I'm saying, get over it and get to work! *(GEORGIA returns to center stage.)* Come on, Romeo. Let's pick it up from "But soft."

DAVE. Places top of II-2. *(WENDY walks to the back of the house. GEORGIA steps up onto the cubes DAVE has stacked.)* Curtain.

CHRIS as ROMEO.

But soft! What light through yonder window breaks?
It is the east, and Juliet is the sun!
Arise, fair sun, and kill the envious moon,
Who is already sick and pale with grief,
That thou her maid art far more fair than she:
(He pauses, groping for a line. He repeats.)
That thou her maid art far more fair than she...
(He breaks.) Damn it.

DAVE *(prompting CHRIS)*. "Be not her maid, since she is envious"
CHRIS *(to DAVE)*. I know the line. *(To GEORGIA.)* Will you stop looking at me?
GEORGIA. What?
CHRIS *(to WENDY)*. Juliet hasn't entered yet.
GEORGIA. Well, pretend I'm not here.
CHRIS. Can't she be offstage?
GEORGIA. What is your problem?
CHRIS. Stop looking at me.
DAVE. Come on, guys. You're not in kindergarten.
WENDY. Quiet. Georgia, stand with your back to him until your entrance. Chris, pick it up from where you left off.
CHRIS *(shakes himself out, hard, in an attempt to rid himself of the anger and frustration)*. Okay, okay.
DAVE *(prompting CHRIS)*. "Be not her maid, since she is envious"
CHRIS. I know. I know. *(He does a quick vocal exercise.)* Hmmmmm-AH. Hmmmmmmm-Ah. Okay, okay.

CHRIS as ROMEO.
    Be not her maid, since she is envious:
    Her vestal livery is but sick and green,
    And none but fools do wear it; cast if off.
  (GEORGIA turns to him, indicating her entrance.)
    It is my lady; O! *(Groping for a line.)* It is my lady;
    O!... Oh, boy, it is my lady.

GEORGIA *(prompting CHRIS)*. "It is my love"
CHRIS. You want to do this part?
GEORGIA. Dag. I was just...
CHRIS. I know the friggin' line. Just give me a minute.

DAVE. Let's pick it up from, "It is my lady"
WENDY *(coming to the stage and sitting down).* No, Dave, wait. Okay, guys, what's going on?
DAVE. We're never going to get through this.

(LORRAINE enters from the back of the house with coffee.)

WENDY. When I need your advice, I'll ask for it.
LORRAINE. Coffee time! Looks like I'm right on cue. I got an extra black coffee for you, G.
GEORGIA. Hah! Hah!
LORRAINE. I mean an *additional* black coffee.
WENDY *(grabbing her coffee).* God, I need this. What time is it? Dave, call Mercutio, Benvolio and the Friar. We're not going to get to them. Tag them onto tomorrow's rehearsal.
DAVE. That's what I said twenty minutes ago. I don't know if I can catch them home now.
WENDY. Well try hard. Then take ten for yourself while I talk with these guys.
DAVE. Shouldn't I be here?
WENDY. I'll call you when I need you.
DAVE. You're making all this harder than it has to be. *(WENDY shoots him a look. DAVE exits.)*
WENDY. We're going to work this out.
LORRAINE. I'll be in the back.
WENDY. No, sit down, Lorraine. I think you can help. *(To CHRIS and GEORGIA.)* Unless you two can fall in love within the next ten minutes, the whole production is going down the toilet. What's it going to take?
CHRIS. Georgia learning her lines.

GEORGIA. I told you, I'll know them by tomorrow.
WENDY. It's not just the lines. You two are going to have to *pretend* to fall in love. How can you pull that off when you're at each other's throats? *(GEORGIA and CHRIS are hostile and quiet.)* Lorraine, can you help me out here?
LORRAINE. Georgia, why are you acting so evil?
GEORGIA. So it's all my fault.
LORRAINE *(to CHRIS).* And you're like an alley cat on a barbed-wire fence.
GEORGIA. He's all coked up.
CHRIS *(exploding).* That's a lie! I'm clean and you know it!
LORRAINE. He is clean.
GEORGIA. I'm tired of being his therapy.
CHRIS *(to WENDY).* You know I'm clean.
WENDY. I know. Georgia, that wasn't fair.
LORRAINE *(to CHRIS as she massages his shoulders).* Take it easy.
GEORGIA. So it's blame Georgia for everything.
WENDY. Oh come on, G. How many shows have we done together? "As You Like It," "You Can't Take it With You," "Merry Wives of Windsor," "A Member of the Wedding"...
GEORGIA. Wenches, maids, sidekicks and floozies, that's me.
WENDY. Exactly. You never got a shot at leading lady. I never got a shot at directing Shakespeare. So you and I fought for this all the way up to the Board. And now we're here. What do we do?
CHRIS. She's scared. This is her first leading role and she's throwing her guts up.

GEORGIA. It has nothing to do with that.

CHRIS. Well it's my first one too, babe. Grow up, and learn your lines.

GEORGIA. You've only done seven outta your twelve steps, boy. Don't be telling me what to do.

CHRIS. Then stop putting me back on coke.

GEORGIA. I don't have to put up with this. I got enough on my mind.

WENDY. That's *my* point. Whatever you're bringing in from outside is affecting your work, Georgia. If this continues...

GEORGIA. What? You gonna replace me?

WENDY *(surprised)*. No. I was going to say that we'll have to delay the opening. *(Silence. Everyone thinks about what GEORGIA has said.)*

LORRAINE. Can I make a suggestion?

WENDY. I wish you would.

LORRAINE. I think we need to separate the work stuff from the personal stuff. How much time do we have left in here?

WENDY. The schedule's all messed up now. We've got to be out in a little while so the set guys can come in.

LORRAINE. Then let's work now. No breaks. Just keep running and running, no matter what. Afterwards, we all do coffee at Chino's and work out the other stuff.

(DAVE enters, unseen by the cast.)

GEORGIA. I can't be hanging out in Chino's all night. I gotta work tomorrow morning. I ain't rich.

CHRIS. Is that what's bugging you? You want me to take a job at McDonalds, now?

LORRAINE. He can't help who his father is.

WENDY. I'm going to separate you. Lorraine and Georgia, run Nurse/Juliet II-5 with me. Chris, run lines with Dave backstage.

CHRIS. Much as I run lines with Dave, he should be Juliet.

DAVE. Don't you think they should...

WENDY. Did you reach the others?

DAVE. All except for Mercutio. I told the others tomorrow at five.

WENDY. You know I'm not here until six.

DAVE. I'll work with them until you get here.

WENDY *(clearly annoyed, barely restraining herself)*. No. I want you to call them back and tell them six. Then run lines with Chris backstage as I asked.

DAVE. Can I talk to you a minute?

WENDY. I don't have time now.

DAVE *(taking her aside)*. Make time. *(CHRIS and LORRAINE move aside and speak to each other privately. GEORGIA exits quickly through the house.)* You keep separating them and they'll never work together. *(Enthusiastic about his idea.)* Let Chris watch Georgia. She's brilliant playing off of Lorraine. It will build up his confidence in her.

WENDY. No. With Chris watching, she'll pull back and he'll gloat.

DAVE. She won't pull back. She's got too much pride.

WENDY. No.

DAVE. You're demoralizing Chris.

WENDY. We're going to do it my way, Dave. You have a problem with that?

DAVE. I'm just trying to...

WENDY. ...*Direct*, I know. But I'm the director and we're going to do it my way.
DAVE. I just want the show to be good.
WENDY. Then stop hassling me.
DAVE. You just don't get it.
WENDY *(pointing her finger at him)*. No, *you* just don't get it. *(She walks away from him abruptly).* Juliet and Nurse, places for II-5. *(DAVE and CHRIS exit backstage. WENDY waits, then:)* Dave's gonna go to the Board behind my back.
LORRAINE. No, he won't.
WENDY. Unless you and Georgia help me pull this out, I'm in deep trouble. Shakespeare is the season moneymaker. We're sold out the entire first week. If I blow this, they'll never let me direct Shakespeare again. That's what Dave's counting on.
LORRAINE. You treat him like a dog. All he wants to do is help you.
WENDY. I don't think so.
LORRAINE. I thought the Scottish play was supposed to have all the bad luck. This thing has us all at each other's throats. I've never loved a play more and wanted to rehearse it less.
WENDY. All we can do is work. Let's hit it. Places for II-2. *(Looking around.)* Where the heck is Georgia now?
LORRAINE. Pay phone.
WENDY. I don't believe it! *(Shouting.)* Georgia! *(To LORRAINE.)* Will you tell me what's wrong with her?
LORRAINE. Jimmy's putting a lot of pressure on her.
WENDY. He's always tried to get her to quit theatre, but she handled it.
LORRAINE. I think it's really bad this time.

WENDY. He waits till I'm finally directing her to act like a number one idiot. Why did I pick Shakespeare? Why did I say I wanted to direct? Why am I in the theatre?

LORRAINE. You don't want me to answer any of that.

WENDY. No.

LORRAINE. Good, 'cause you're depressing me. You know you were born to direct this. It's Juliet's play and you know how to make it work.

WENDY. Dave would have pumped Romeo full of testosterone...

LORRAINE. ...and Juliet full of saccharine.

WENDY. I know what I'm doing.

LORRAINE. Of course you do. Stop letting Dave intimidate you.

WENDY. It's going to be fine.

LORRAINE. It's going to be great!

WENDY. You're a fabulous actor, Lorraine. You almost had me believing that. *(Shouting.)* Georgia! *(To LORRAINE.)* Look, jump into II-5 as soon as she comes back. Tease her, schtick it up if you have to. Take her mind off Jimmy and build up her confidence.

LORRAINE. I'll do my best.

(GEORGIA enters.)

WENDY. Places, II-5. *(GEORGIA is preoccupied and does not respond.)* Places, II-5.

GEORGIA. I don't think I can do this.

LORRAINE *(taking GEORGIA by the arm)*. Did you speak to Jimmy?

GEORGIA. The machine's on. We fought before I left.

LORRAINE. You worried about him? *(GEORGIA nods. She is on the verge of tears.)*

GEORGIA. I don't know where he is.

LORRAINE. Well, Juliet don't know where the nurse is either. Use it! *(GEORGIA looks at her.)* Use it! Come on!

(LORRAINE pulls GEORGIA onstage. GEORGIA starts the monologue. Although still somewhat stiff and preoccupied in the beginning, we see her begin to use her own anxiety and plug it into Juliet's. By the end of her monologue we should see her as quite a touching anxious Juliet.)

GEORGIA as JULIET.
>The clock struck nine when I did send the nurse'
>In half an hour she promised to return.
>Perchance she cannot meet him: that's not so.
>O! She is lame: love's heralds should be thoughts
>Which ten times faster glide than the sun's beams
>Driving back shadows over lowring hills:
>Therefore do nimble-pinion'd doves draw Love,
>And therefore hath the wind-swift Cupid wings.
>Now is the sun upon the highmost hill
>Of this day's journey, and from nine till twelve
>Is three long hours, yet she is not come.
>Had she affections, and warm youthful blood,
>She'd be as swift in motion as a ball:
>My words would bandy her to my sweet love,
>And his to me:
>But old folks, many feign as they were dead;
>Unwieldy, slow, heavy and pale as lead.

(Enter LORRAINE as NURSE.)

JULIET.
> O God! she comes. O honey nurse! what news?
> Hast thou met with him?
> Now, good sweet nurse; O Lord! why lookst thou
>   sad?
> Though news be sad, yet tell them merrily;
> If good, thou shamest the music of sweet news
> By playing it to me with so sour a face.

LORRAINE as NURSE.
> I am aweary, give me leave awhile:
> Fie, how my bones ache! What a jaunce have I had!

JULIET.
> I wouldst thou hadst my bones, and I thy news:
> Nay, come, I pray thee, speak: good, good nurse,
>   speak.

NURSE.
> Jesu! what haste; can you not stay awhile?
> Do you not see that I am out of breath?

JULIET *(GEORGIA plays this very angrily)*.
> How art thou out of breath when thou hast breath
> To say to me that thou art out of breath?
> The excuse that thou dost make in this delay
> Is longer than the tale thou dost excuse.
> Is thy news good, or bad? answer to that'
> *(GEORGIA smacks LORRAINE on the shoulder.)*
> Answer to that;

PLAYING JULIET

    Say either, and I'll stay the circumstance:
    Let me be satisfied, is't good or bad?

LORRAINE. Ow!
GEORGIA. Sorry.
WENDY. Take out that slap, Georgia.
LORRAINE *(rubbing her arm)*. Thank you.
GEORGIA. But she's really angry.
WENDY. More impatient than angry here.
LORRAINE. And the nurse would slap her down.
WENDY. Keep going.
GEORGIA. But I think the nurse has spoiled her and...
WENDY. KEEP GOING! Your line, Nurse!

(LORRAINE begins with gusto. GEORGIA sulks. She clearly has difficulty accepting the direction WENDY has given her.)

NURSE.
    Well you have made a simple choice; you know not how to choose a man: Romeo! no, not he; though his face be better than any man's yet his leg excels all men's; and for a hand, and a foot, and a body, though they not be talked on, yet they are past compare. He is not the flower of courtesy, but, I'll warrant him, as gentle as a lamb. Go thy ways, wench; serve God. What! have you dined at home?

JULIET *(GEORGIA delivers this sulkily)*.
    No, no; but all this I did know before.
    What says he of our marriage? What of that?

WENDY. You should be eager, Juliet.

NURSE.
>Lord! how my head aches; what a head have I!
>It beats as it would fall in twenty pieces.
>My back o' t'other side; O! my back, my back.

WENDY. Massage her here, Juliet.
GEORGIA. But I'm angry with her.
WENDY. Just do it. Keep going. *(GEORGIA reluctantly massages the NURSE.)*

NURSE.
>Beshrew your heart for sending me about,
>To catch my death with jauncing up and down.

JULIET.
>I' faith, I am sorry that thou art not well.
>Sweet, sweet, sweet nurse, tell me, what says my love.

WENDY. That's not sarcasm, Juliet. You really coddle Nurse here.
GEORGIA. Why?
LORRAINE. Just do it.
GEORGIA. I can't do it if I don't know why.
LORRAINE. Finish the scene.
WENDY. Keep going.

NURSE.
>Your love says like an honest gentleman, and a courteous, and a kind and a handsome, and I warrant, a virtuous...

(LORRAINE pauses because GEORGIA is crying.)

WENDY. KEEP GOING!

NURSE.
　...Where is your mother!

JULIET *(GEORGIA is crying but saying the lines).*
　Where is my mother! Why she is within;
　Where should she be?

WENDY *(frustrated).* Hold it! Georgia, this sets up the comic bit. It's supposed to be funny. I mean, I'm open to new interpretations, but this is supposed to be a warm, comic exchange.

GEORGIA. I'm sorry. I can't do this.

LORRAINE. Yes you can. Let's take it again from the top.

GEORGIA. No. I can't. *(She goes to get her bag and coat.)*

LORRAINE. Where do you think you're going?

GEORGIA. Home.

WENDY. Home?!

LORRAINE *(to GEORGIA).* What is with you? You are beyond bizarre. This is a break any of us would kill for.

GEORGIA. That's an idea. Kill me, and the part is yours.

LORRAINE. Why are choking on this? You turned it out in auditions.

WENDY. This is the scene that got you the part.

GEORGIA. Why did you cast me as Juliet?

WENDY. What??

GEORGIA. You heard me.

WENDY. Because you are a perfect Juliet.

GEORGIA. What are you trying to prove?

LORRAINE. Everybody's fighting demons, Chris.
CHRIS. Why did you shoot me down when I asked you out?
LORRAINE. You had an attitude.
CHRIS. My hands were shaking.
LORRAINE. You came on like a spoiled brat. You assumed I would say yes because your father's on the Board. I don't want you thinking you can buy me.
CHRIS. You wouldn't even let me drive you home.
LORRAINE. You know what would happen to you and your little red Mazda on my street?
WENDY. Hey, guys. This is really touching, but I've got twenty minutes to pull this scene together.
GEORGIA. Come on, Lorraine. Take Juliet. You've wanted it all along.
LORRAINE *(turning squarely to GEORGIA).* Sometimes I ask myself why I bother to try to be your friend. I'm so tired of the grief, Georgia. How long have we known each other? When are you going to forgive me for being lighter than you? Huh? What do I have to do to prove my friendship? Here I am, a wannabe famous actor, willing to give up the leading-lady role of all time for you. I didn't even audition.
GEORGIA. So you're saying if you had auditioned I wouldn't have gotten the role?
LORRAINE. No, stupid! I'm saying I didn't want to compete with you. What else do I have to do to prove myself to you? *(Silence.)*
WENDY. I had no idea all this was going on.
DAVE. I did.
WENDY *(with heavy sarcasm).* I'm sure you did. Resident genius and psychologist that you are. *(Back to GEOR-*

GIA.) Georgia, I cast you because you are a talented and consummately beautiful Juliet.

GEORGIA. Come on, Wendy. I am not beautiful.

LORRAINE. What are you saying?

GEORGIA. Ask your sister. She'll explain.

LORRAINE. You and Liz have your little club, from which I am excluded.

GEORGIA *(sarcastically)*. Poor you. You get all the guys. So don't begrudge us our little darkies club.

LORRAINE. This color thing is nonsense and you know it. I was born this way. Do you think that makes my life free of pain?

DAVE. Both of you are beautiful.

WENDY. Oh shut up, Dave.

DAVE. No, Wendy. They're my friends too. *(To GEORGIA and LORRAINE.)* You're both beautiful women.

GEORGIA. Don't even say "classic African features."

DAVE. But it's true.

GEORGIA. Juliet wasn't no African and Shakespeare is very clear about what she looks like. Romeo says...

"The brightness of her cheek would shame those stars"
and...

"On the white wonder of dear Juliet's hand"
How am I supposed to deliver a line like...

"Thou know'st the mask of night is on my face
Else would a maiden blush bepaint my cheek."
They'll laugh me off the stage. And he's real clear about what black means too.

"So shows a snowy dove trooping with crows
As yonder lady o'er her fellow shows"
White is beautiful. Black is ugly.

WENDY. But Juliet sings praises to the blackness of night,

"Spread thy close curtain, love-performing night..."
and...
"Come gentle night, come loving, black-browed night..."
Georgia, we're not being literal, this is poetry.

DAVE. I'm so tired of this color thing.

GEORGIA. You think *you're* tired?!

WENDY. This play shows a universal beauty that's far more than skin deep. I've always seen you in this role. My beautiful Juliet *is* black.

GEORGIA. It won't work.

LORRAINE. How can you be so blind to your own beauty? How can we make you see it?

CHRIS. You can't. Nobody can do that for her. She's got to believe in herself first. *(To GEORGIA, lightly.)* Excuse a little seven- out of twelve-step philosophy.

GEORGIA *(turning on CHRIS)*. Why do you always struggle with those lines?

CHRIS. What lines?

GEORGIA *(quoting Romeo)*.
> "It seems she hangs upon the cheek of night
> Like a rich jewel in an Ethiope's ear;
> Beauty too rich for use, for earth too dear!"

CHRIS. I struggle with all my lines. My brain is toast. I haven't been in front of a live audience in years. My old man sits on your Board. My struggles have nothing to do with your looks or your color. I'm getting nothing but hostility from you.

WENDY. My Juliet is courageous despite her vulnerability. She defies her family. She faces danger and death. There's a heck of a woman in that young girl's body.

GEORGIA. And of course I've got a young girl's body.

WENDY. No, but Chris isn't seventeen either. This is theatre, people. It's illusion, it's poetry.
LORRAINE. Georgia, don't let us down.
GEORGIA. It's not just about you.
WENDY. Jimmy? *(GEORGIA nods.)*
DAVE. Maybe if he saw you act...
GEORGIA. He's never come to any of my shows. He definitely won't have anything to do with this. He doesn't want me acting.
WENDY. That's never stopped you before.
GEORGIA *(sobbing).* He says if I do this part, he'll leave me. He says I'll disgrace myself and humiliate him.
WENDY. This is the greatest role of all time! Why would he say that?
GEORGIA. I don't know. All we do is scream at each other. I only know that if I do this part, he will leave me.
DAVE. You have to do it.
WENDY. We need you.
LORRAINE. You have to do this for yourself.
GEORGIA. I love him so much.
LORRAINE. Then he's got to love who and what you are.
WENDY. Can't you speak to him?
GEORGIA. I've used up all the words I know.
WENDY. Fight for him. Tell him how much you love him.
GEORGIA. How?
WENDY. Act III, Scene 5.
GEORGIA. What?
WENDY. Do it.
GEORGIA. Now?
WENDY. Right now. Dave, give her a line.
GEORGIA. I can't. I'm a mess.

WENDY. So is Juliet. Chris, go to her. *(CHRIS gives LORRAINE a quick kiss on the lips, then approaches GEORGIA.)* It is daybreak, Juliet. After your night of passionate lovemaking, Romeo has to go.

GEORGIA. I can't do it, Wendy.

WENDY. The one man you love in all the world is slipping out of your hands. Hold on to him. Put her arms around you, Chris. *(CHRIS does so.)* Go on, Georgia. Use the poetry to bind him to you.

DAVE *(prompting GEORGIA).* "Wilt thou be gone?" *(Pause. He repeats the prompt.)* "Wilt thou be gone?" *(GEORGIA sighs, but begins to say Juliet's lines, balancing her own personal grief with the joy she feels for acting.)*

GEORGIA as JULIET.
> Wilt thou be gone? it is not yet near day:
> It was the nightingale, and not the lark,
> That pierc'd the fearful hollow of thine ear;
> Nightly she sings on yon pomegranate tree:
> Believe me, love, it was the nightingale.

WENDY. Try to get out of there, Romeo. Make her see reality.

CHRIS as ROMEO.
> It was the lark, the herald of the morn,
> No nightingale: look, love, what envious streaks
> Do lace the severing clouds in yonder east:
> Night's candles are burnt out, and jocund day
> Stands tiptoe on the misty mountain tops:
> I must be gone and live, or stay and die.

JULIET *(clings to ROMEO passionately).*
>Yon light is not daylight, I know it, I:
>It is some meteor that the sun exhales,
>To be to thee this night a torch-bearer,
>And light thee on thy way to Mantua:
>Therefore stay yet; thou needs't not to be gone.

WENDY. Good. But Juliet has to let him go or he'll be killed.

DAVE *(prompting her).* "It is, it is; hie hence, be gone, away!"

JULIET.
>It is, it is; hie hence, be gone, away!
>It is the lark that sings so out of tune,
>Straining harsh discords and unpleasing sharps.
>Some say the lark makes sweet division;
>This doth not so, for she divideth us:
>*(She starts to cry. She lets CHRIS hold her tenderly.)*
>O'now be gone; more light and light it grows.

ROMEO.
>More light and light; more dark and dark our woes!

JULIET *(clinging to ROMEO).*
>O God, I have an ill-divining soul.
>Methinks I see thee, now thou art below,
>As one dead in the bottom of a tomb:
>Either my eyesight fails, or thou look'st pale.

ROMEO *(leaving her, tenderly).*
>And trust me, love, in my eye so do you:
>Dry sorrow drinks our blood. Adieu, adieu!

WENDY. Juliet's premonition proves correct. Skip ahead to the tomb. Chris, lay down over there. *(CHRIS lies down with his back to her, as if dead.)* Juliet, you discover Romeo, laying there before you, dead.

DAVE *(prompting GEORGIA)*. Act V, Scene 3 death speech.

WENDY. Start from where you are with Jimmy.

GEORGIA. I'm not pretending Jimmy's dead. No way.

WENDY. Of course not. Imagine Jimmy sleeping. Tell him what is in your heart.

(GEORGIA is still unsure about following WENDY's lead into the improvisation. A pause. She closes her eyes and imagines JIMMY. CHRIS remains immobile as GEORGIA begins speaking softly with her eyes closed.)

GEORGIA.
 Jimmy.
 Tell me you haven't closed your heart to me.
 I love you.
 My need for you is so deep. More than water.
 More than food.
 But how can I love you if you will not let me breathe?
 I am no beauty. I know that. I am black and plain.
 Don't you know how I long to be beautiful for you?
 Let me crown myself in Juliet's beauty;
 Let me borrow her beautiful words;
 Let me, just once in my life, feel that I have earned your love.
 Won't you love me?
 Won't you let me love you?

WENDY. Romeo is dead, Juliet.

DAVE *(prompting)*. "What's here? a cup..."

GEORGIA as JULIET.
>What's here? a cup closed in my true love's hand?
>Poison, I see, hath been his timeless end.
>O churl! drunk all, and left no friendly drop
>To help me after! I will kiss thy lips;
>Haply some poison yet doth hang on them,
>To make me die with a restorative.
>Thy lips are warm!
>Yea, noise? then I'll be brief. O happy dagger!
>This is thy sheath;
>There rust, and let me die!

(GEORGIA lets out a gut-wrenching howl, collapses and lies still for a beat. Silence. Suddenly we hear someone clapping. JIMMY approaches the stage from the back of the house. He comes into the light, startling everyone. He is truly moved.)

GEORGIA. Jimmy!

JIMMY. Wow!

GEORGIA. How did you get here?

JIMMY. Baby, you were great. It's not like I understand everything you said and all... But you're...so good.

GEORGIA. I can't believe you're here.

JIMMY. There was a message on the machine from some guy named Dave.

DAVE. That would be me.

GEORGIA *(remembering that JIMMY doesn't know people)*. Oh, Jimmy, this is Dave. This is Wendy.

WENDY. Hi, we've spoken on the phone.

GEORGIA. You know Lorraine.

LORRAINE. So we finally got you inside a theatre.

GEORGIA. And this is Chris.

CHRIS. How's it going?

JIMMY. Right.

GEORGIA *(to DAVE)*. You called Jimmy?

JIMMY. He said you were sick.

GEORGIA. I was.

JIMMY. Said I should come down here to take you home.

DAVE. I hoped to convince him to watch some of the rehearsal. I knew he'd understand if he could see your work.

WENDY. Isn't she a wonderful Juliet?

JIMMY *(suddenly shy)*. Can we go somewhere to talk?

GEORGIA. They need to know what I'm going to do, Jimmy.

JIMMY *(hesitates, but speaks despite his discomfort)*. Georgia, don't you know that you are the most beautiful woman on this planet?

GEORGIA. You said I would humiliate you if I did this role.

JIMMY. 'Cause I didn't want the woman I love slobbering all over some white boy. All you talk about is "Chris this, Chris that." You got some rich white boy playing Romeo to your Juliet, and I'm supposed to like it?

GEORGIA. It's just a part in a play.

JIMMY. All you do is talk about him.

GEORGIA. Because I can't stand him.

CHRIS. Thanks.

GEORGIA. Why would you be jealous of him when all I did was say how much I hated him?

JIMMY. Yeah, but hate that strong has got to have love on the other side. Like Beatrice and Benedick.

WENDY *(surprised)*. What?

JIMMY. In the video.

GEORGIA. When did you see "Much Ado About Nothing"? When I rented it, you refused to watch it with me.

JIMMY. I rented it by myself. I didn't want to be sitting up there with you, not knowing what they were saying. But when I saw it, I got madder at you. 'Cause Beatrice was always talking about how she hates Benedick when all the time she's got a thing for him. So you're in rehearsal with this rich white boy all night long and you're talking about how much you hate him all the time. Doesn't take a genius to figure out how that will go.

GEORGIA. But this is *Romeo and Juliet*.

JIMMY. That's what I said. Okay, she ain't doin' this play, she's doing the other one. So I rented it. Lord, why'd I have to do that? Talk about two different houses. That's a trip. I'm looking at Juliet's father and seeing yours. You know he doesn't think I'm good enough for you. Wouldn't he like you bringing home some rich boy?! Then Romeo and Juliet start rolling around in bed, buck naked. Now you know I'm going to have to hurt me somebody up in here.

GEORGIA. But I want you!

CHRIS *(indicating LORRAINE)*. I want her.

LORRAINE *(indicating CHRIS)*. I want him.

WENDY. And they're not buck naked!

GEORGIA. How long were you watching us?

JIMMY. I heard you threaten to quit. I heard what you said to him when you were pretending it was me. That hurt me.

GEORGIA *(shocked)*. Hurt you?! Why?

JIMMY. How could you say that you are black and plain. Don't you know how beautiful you are? What good is my love if I can't make you feel beautiful? That's why I get mad about you coming down here all the time, messing with this acting. It's like my love is never enough to make you feel beautiful.

GEORGIA. But without your love, I'd never have the courage to do it. I can take the biggest risk in the world if I know you love me. Your love makes me strong. I'd walk away from this rather than lose you.

JIMMY. No. No. Don't quit. You're really good. I mean, I'm never going to like you kissing him. But, you're too good to quit.

GEORGIA. I love you so much. *(They embrace. The others are moved by their love and make sympathetic sounds.)* It's okay, then?

JIMMY. Just keep your clothes on and don't fall in love with the white boy.

CHRIS. The white boy's name is Chris, by the way.

LORRAINE. And he's spoken for.

WENDY. So, can we work now? *(LORRAINE, CHRIS, GEORGIA and JIMMY make approving sounds. WENDY gives a sigh of relief.)*

GEORGIA *(to the group).* I know I haven't been easy to work with. *(She searches for the words.)* I...I...don't know if you can understand how I feel. This is a complicated time in my life.

LORRAINE. We love you, Georgia. Sometimes we don't know why, but we do.

GEORGIA. I'm really ready to do this now.

DAVE *(looking at his watch).* The set crew will be here any minute.

WENDY. We're out of time, people. Starting tomorrow, we work like dogs. *(People start preparing to leave, putting clothing and scripts in their bags, finishing water, etc. WENDY and DAVE move to opposite sides of the stage. WENDY gets buried in her script, making notes. DAVE replaces set pieces and checks his "To Do" list and barks orders at the actors.)*

DAVE. Call is for five on the dot and you will be fined for lateness. Sneak out of work if you have to. Pick up your trash. Take all your stuff with you.

CHRIS. I'll wait for you outside.

LORRAINE. You can drop me at my house.

CHRIS. Oh. I thought you could... come over to my place and... and...

LORRAINE. You wanna "and" already, huh? Well, won't be no "and" tonight. Just slow down. If you can beat off the muggers when you drop me at *my place*, if you can figure out how to introduce me to your father without him having a heart attack, then maybe we can talk about "and."

CHRIS *(lightly)*. You're a hard woman, Lorraine.

LORRAINE. Uh-huh! Just what you need, too. *(CHRIS and LORRAINE begin to exit.)*

CHRIS. See you all tomorrow.

JIMMY *(teasing)*. Hey, Chris, don't make me have to come looking for you. *(CHRIS looks worried.)* Just kidding you, man.

CHRIS *(uncertainly)*. I knew that.

GEORGIA *(teasing LORRAINE)*. Don't hurt yourselves, now.

LORRAINE. Likewise. *(CHRIS and LORRAINE exit.)*

WENDY. Dave, call Friar Lawrence, Benvolio, Mercutio. Tell them we start at five tomorrow.

DAVE. I thought you couldn't be here until six.

WENDY. We'll start at five with a run-through.

DAVE. A run-through?

WENDY. Am I not speaking English? *(A tense silence.)*

JIMMY *(examining one of the set pieces)*. What's this?

DAVE. It'll be part of the balcony, if we can get the rest of the wood.

JIMMY. You gonna brace these joints?

DAVE. I guess.

GEORGIA. Jimmy does carpentry, electronics, plumbing, you name it.

JIMMY. I just mess around.

GEORGIA. You know you're good.

DAVE. Know where we can get some cheap two by four?

JIMMY. Maybe.

WENDY. Georgia, why don't you show him around the theatre?

GEORGIA. Wanna look around?

JIMMY. Sure.

GEORGIA. Just go in there and take a right into the little office. I gotta do something first. I'll be right there. *(JIMMY exits backstage.)*

DAVE. The printer's coming at five tomorrow. I'll proof the program.

WENDY. I want to see it. Nothing goes out of here without my approval.

GEORGIA *(to WENDY)*. Thank you for having so much faith in me.

WENDY. You're going to be terrific.

GEORGIA *(to DAVE)*. And if it wasn't for your message, Jimmy never would have set foot in here.

DAVE. No problem.

GEORGIA. Actually, there's still one more problem.

WENDY. What now?

GEORGIA *(indicates WENDY and DAVE)*. The two of you. Everybody else has been making friends tonight.

WENDY. We're all right.

GEORGIA. The whole cast is talking about it. Mommy and Daddy shouldn't fight in front of the kids.

DAVE. I'm doing my job, but I get on her nerves.

GEORGIA. What about it, Wendy? *(After a pause.)*

WENDY. He's always in my face. I've got too much on my mind.

DAVE. A stage manager is supposed to take some of the weight.

WENDY. Take weight, not take over. Did your stage manager give you notes?

DAVE. I'm sorry.

GEORGIA *(prompting WENDY)*. He said he's sorry.

WENDY. Okay.

GEORGIA *(to WENDY)*. Is that all you can say? For somebody so smart about directing, you sure can be dumb about life. Can't you see he's crazy about you?

WENDY. What?

GEORGIA *(knocking on WENDY's head as if it were hollow)*. Hello? You're defensive because you're intimidated by his experience. You've got a crush on him turned inside out. You think he wants your job. But he wants you. *(She leaves an embarrassed WENDY and crosses directly to DAVE.)* And for somebody so neat and organized, you sure need to get your act together. Why don't you tell the woman how you feel about her? *(GEORGIA snatches DAVE's things out of his hands.)* She thinks you're spying on her for the Board.

DAVE. That's absurd! The Board's been pressuring me to take over but I'm sticking up for her.

GEORGIA. Tell her the real reason you're in her face all the time.

DAVE *(after a pause)*. She wouldn't be interested.

GEORGIA. Well, you're the Shakespeare expert. He knew how to talk that talk. *(As she quotes the play, she takes DAVE by the arm and moves him close to WENDY.)*
 "But passion lends them power, time means, to meet,
 Tempering extremities with extreme sweet."
(GEORGIA exits backstage, leaving WENDY and DAVE mute, rooted to the spot and unable to look at each other. After a few beats, DAVE speaks.)

DAVE. So call's at five o'clock, right?

WENDY. Right.

DAVE. Right. *(Silence.)*

WENDY. I *can* do this show, Dave.

DAVE. I know.

WENDY. It's like you don't think I know what I'm doing.

DAVE. I never could have gotten this kind of work out of the actors. You're incredible.

WENDY. Don't second-guess me.

DAVE. I was only offering some suggestions...

WENDY. Wait till I ask.

DAVE. I'm sorry. When I've got a lot to do I get...

WENDY. ...hyper? pushy? aggressive?

DAVE. All of the above. Sorry. *(Silence.)*

WENDY. You're a wonderful SM. If it wasn't for you, I wouldn't have a Juliet right now. I'll try not to be so...

DAVE. Hyper, pushy, aggressive? *(WENDY smiles.)* What Georgia said... is it true? ... a "crush... turned inside out"?

WENDY *(suddenly getting busy)*. You can proof the program. I'm going to stop obsessing about it. You can work II-1 with Benvolio and...

DAVE. Is it true? *(Silence.)*

WENDY. Did you really stick up for me with the Board?

DAVE *(quoting Juliet III-2).* "Did ever dragon keep so fair a cave?"

WENDY. What?

DAVE. "Beautiful tyrant!"

WENDY. Does that mean yes?

DAVE. "Fiend angelical!"

WENDY. Don't play games.

DAVE. "Dove-feathered raven! Wolvish-ravening lamb!"

WENDY. Tell me before I make a fool of myself!

DAVE. Will you be my Viola in "Twelfth Night"? I'm proposing it to the Board for next season.

WENDY. Will you be my Iago? If I pull this off, I'm proposing "Othello."

DAVE. Are you crazy? We could never do a show like that.

WENDY. That's exactly why I want to do it.

DAVE. I'm going to fight you over this.

WENDY. I'd expect nothing less. *(He kisses her. She quotes Juliet.)* "... although I joy in thee,

It is too rash, too unadvised, too sudden."

DAVE *(quoting Romeo).* "O, wilt though leave me so unsatisfied?"

WENDY *(quoting Juliet).* "What satisfaction canst thou have tonight?"

DAVE. Whatever you want... I just...

(This time, she kisses him. GEORGIA and JIMMY enter, just in time to see WENDY and DAVE fly apart and get very busy.)

WENDY. So if you work II-1...

DAVE. Sure, sure. I can work the other scene. *(DAVE and WENDY are flustered.)*

WENDY. I'm out of here. You guys going?

GEORGIA. Jimmy wants to meet the carpenters.

DAVE. I'll walk you out. I mean, I'm going that way anyway.

WENDY. Sure. Okay. Right. Well, good night.

JIMMY. See you.

GEORGIA. See you tomorrow. *(DAVE and WENDY exit.)*

JIMMY *(grabbing a script)*. What's up with that?

GEORGIA. We'll see.

JIMMY *(taking stage)*. Move over, Denzel Washington! Move over, Larry Fishburne! Jimmy's in the house! *(Quoting Romeo.)* "Here's to my love! O true apothecary!
   Thy drugs are quick. Thus with a kiss I die."
   (JIMMY falls dramatically on the ground.)

GEORGIA. Well look at you.

JIMMY. And we can practice your love scenes at home. Watched the video three times. Tell me Juliet's father ain't just like yours. Tell me we ain't the star-crossed lovers.

GEORGIA. They defied their parents and married anyway.

JIMMY. And see how they ended up. We're just living together and I'm looking over my shoulder all the time. A college professor with a maintenance man for a son-in-law? Please. If I tried to marry you, your father would take out a contract on me.

GEORGIA. He might disown me, but he wouldn't hurt you.

JIMMY. You don't know that.

GEORGIA *(quoting Juliet)*.

"If that thy bent of love be honorable,

Thy purpose marriage, send me word tomorrow

And all my fortunes at thy foot I'll lay

And follow thee my lord throughout the world."

JIMMY. Translation?

GEORGIA. If you saw the video three times, you know what I said.

JIMMY. You were the one who said we should wait.

GEORGIA. It's different now.

JIMMY. Because you're going to be acting?

GEORGIA. No. Because I... Look, let's go home. I've got something to tell you.

JIMMY. What?

GEORGIA. Not here.

JIMMY. What about the carpenters?

GEORGIA. You can meet them tomorrow. This is more important. *(She starts to exit into the house.)*

JIMMY. But I'm acting.

GEORGIA. Come on, man.

JIMMY *(playing around with a melodramatic reading)*. More light and light; more dark and dark our woes!

GEORGIA. You know how I've been feeling sick in the mornings and throwing up?

JIMMY. Farewell! Farewell! One kiss, and I'll descend.

GEORGIA. Well, I went to the doctor... *(She exits.)*

JIMMY. Farewell!

I will omit no opportunity

That may convey my greetings, love, to thee!

(He notices GEORGIA is gone. He suddenly processes what she has been saying.)

...Hey...wait... Hey...what did you say? *(He runs after her.)* You went to the doctor and what?! Georgia?!

BLACKOUT

CASTING OTHELLO

CHARACTERS

WENDY (plays Desdemona) .... White.

GEORGIA (plays Emilia). .... Dark-skinned African American, 5-6 months pregnant.

LORRAINE (plays Bianca, is also production stage manager) Light-skinned African American.

JIMMY .... African American, husband to Georgia. Maintenance man by profession, does carpentry for the company on a voluntary basis. Tonight he wears a suit.

DAVE (plays Iago) .... White, seasoned actor/director. Slightly older than the others.

CHRIS (plays Cassio, is also director of the production) Young, white.

TIME:
About six months after the events in Part I—*Playing Juliet.*

SETTING.
New Vistas Theatre.

CASTING OTHELLO

SCENE: *New Vistas Theatre. Same setting as for* Playing Juliet.

AT RISE: *The stage is dark except for a work light which creates a spotlight on JIMMY, wearing a suit. He holds the script and does* Othello's *monologue Act V, Scene 2. He performs it simply, as if discovering it. He is moved by the words.*

JIMMY as OTHELLO.
 Soft you. A word or two before you go.
 I have done the state some service, and they know 't.
 No more of that. I pray you in your letters,
 When you shall these unlucky deeds relate,
 Speak of me as I am. Nothing extenuate,
 Nor set down aught in malice. Then must you speak
 Of one that loved not wisely, but too well;
 Of one not easily jealous, but being wrought,
 Perplexed in the extreme; of one whose hand,
 Like the base Judean, threw a pearl away
 Richer than all his tribe; of one whose subdued eyes,
 Albeit unused to the melting mood,
 Drops tears as fast as the Arabian trees
 Their medicinal gum. Set you down this;
 And say besides, that in Aleppo once,

>   Where a malignant and turbanned Turk
>   Beat a Venetian and traduced the state,
>   I took by th' throat the circumcised dog,
>   And smote him thus. *(Pretends to stab himself.)*

LORRAINE *(clapping, speaking from the back of the house).* Bravo. Very impressive!

JIMMY *(startled, somewhat embarrassed).* Hey, Lorraine! I was just messing around.

LORRAINE *(as she walks towards the stage).* Pretty damn good for messing around. Where's Georgia? *(LORRAINE gets out prompt book, starts moving flats and rehearsal cubes.)*

JIMMY. She's coming straight from work. Let me help you.

LORRAINE. Don't mess up your suit. How come you're all dressed up?

JIMMY. Job interview.

LORRAINE. Good luck. You gonna sit through rehearsal again tonight?

JIMMY. Yeah.

LORRAINE. Couldn't get you near a theatre a few months ago. Now we can't get you out.

JIMMY. I guess it grows on you.

LORRAINE. Well, you've been a help. I would have had to walk through the blocking if you weren't here. Jason really screwed us good, taking off for L.A. and leaving us without an Othello.

JIMMY. You don't have anybody yet?

LORRAINE. Chris has some more guys to call tonight.

JIMMY. What if he doesn't find anybody tonight?

LORRAINE. I don't know what the hell we're going to do.

(GEORGIA enters with coffee in hand.)

GEORGIA. I called you at lunch today.
JIMMY. Hey, baby, what's happening? *(Goes to take the coffee away from her.)* Now you know you should *not* be drinking that coffee.
GEORGIA *(snatching back the coffee cup)*. Gimme back my coffee, man, and I thought we had agreed that you'd stay home tonight.
JIMMY. Yeah, well, I just said that to shut you up.
GEORGIA. Where were you at lunch time? I called and called.
JIMMY *(kissing her)*. I told you I had some errands.
GEORGIA. Hey, Lorraine.
LORRAINE. How you feeling, G?
GEORGIA. My back is killing me.
JIMMY. Let me give you a massage.
GEORGIA. No thanks. I want to know what kind of errands you've been running.
JIMMY *(scurries to get a chair)*. Sit down, baby. Doctor says you should stay off your feet.
GEORGIA. I'm fine!
JIMMY. I brought us some dinner. You hungry?
GEORGIA. No.
JIMMY. You eat a healthy lunch? The doctor says you have to ...
GEORGIA. I'm gonna punch you *and* the doctor if you don't stay off my nerves.
LORRAINE. Somebody's evil!
GEORGIA. Mind your business. Chris find an Othello yet?
LORRAINE. Still looking.
GEORGIA. He'd better hurry up.

JIMMY. I could play Othello.
GEORGIA *(not taking him seriously)*. Uh-huh.
JIMMY. I could.
LORRAINE. You've certainly seen it enough, and Lord knows you know the blocking.
GEORGIA. You still haven't answered my question, James. Where have you been taking your lunch hours?
JIMMY. It's a surprise.
GEORGIA. That's just what my left hook's gonna be.
LORRAINE. Ooooh, Jimmy, better watch out.
GEORGIA. And you're next. *(To JIMMY.)* Baby, why don't you come back for me later. You don't need to be hanging around here all night watching rehearsal.
JIMMY. I don't mind. I like doing it.
LORRAINE. I need him to walk through the Act IV, Scene 1 blocking.
GEORGIA. Yeah, but having Jimmy walk through is giving Chris a false sense of security. We need a real Othello.
LORRAINE. He's working on it.
JIMMY. Hey, G? What would you say if I asked Chris about...
GEORGIA. About what? *(We hear the rest of the cast members coming through the back of the house, talking.)*
JIMMY. Never mind.

(CHRIS, DAVE and WENDY enter. The cast members greet each other. A brief moment of chatting, then CHRIS calls everyone to order.)

CHRIS. People, people!
LORRAINE *(loudly)*. Quiet please!

CHRIS. Here's the game plan for tonight. We're going to work IV-1, Cassio, Iago and Othello. Jimmy would you stand in?

JIMMY. Sure!

DAVE. Still no word on a real Othello?

CHRIS. I'm working on it, Dave. Right after we do this scene I've got a list of guys to call. Wendy, a quick warm-up, please. *(The actors get ready for warm-ups. JIMMY joins them.)*

GEORGIA. What do you think you're doing?

JIMMY. Warming up!

GEORGIA. Why?

WENDY. I suggested it. Since he's doing so much reading and all.

GEORGIA *(to JIMMY)*. You're crazy.

WENDY *(leading warm-ups)*. Stretch the arms in the air. Shake out the hands.

DAVE. Why do I hate this?!

LORRAINE. Just do it.

WENDY. Now drop over and touch your toes. Take deep breaths and relax.

JIMMY. Watch out for the baby.

GEORGIA. I'm fine!

WENDY. Now roll up slowly taking deep breaths. Now shake the body loosely as you make sound. *(The cast shakes out, making various sounds.)*

CHRIS. That's fine. Thanks, Wendy.

WENDY. But we just started. We didn't do anything!

CHRIS. I know, but we're way behind schedule.

WENDY. Breathe deeply and pray, people.

LORRAINE. Act IV, Scene 1 in two minutes!

(LORRAINE and CHRIS confer. WENDY does some more quick vocal work, DAVE combs through his script. GEORGIA moves a few chairs and JIMMY rushes in to help her.)

JIMMY. Let me do that, baby.

GEORGIA. I can move a damn chair. *(Pause. JIMMY gets his script. GEORGIA can see he's hurt.)* Jimmy, you gotta go home.

JIMMY. Why?

GEORGIA. You're driving me crazy.

JIMMY. I'm just trying to help.

GEORGIA. You're getting in the way.

JIMMY. Lorraine says she wants me to walk through the blocking.

GEORGIA. Well that's not your job. And you don't have to hang around for me. I keep telling you I'm fine coming home by myself.

JIMMY. I like doing this. I like acting.

GEORGIA. You gotta give me some room, Jimmy. I need room!

WENDY *(approaching JIMMY)*. Jimmy, this is the scene where you're getting real proof. Remember Iago's talking about your bride and your best friend!

GEORGIA. What are you doing?

WENDY. Just...uh...giving him some context.

GEORGIA. Well, he don't need any context. He's just walking through the blocking. Just reading the lines and going home, right? *(GEORGIA storms off to sit on the side, buried in her script. JIMMY shrugs his shoulders, WENDY pats him reassuringly and sits nearby to watch.)*

LORRAINE. All right, people, let's do it! Places IV-1. That's Cassio and Iago with Jimmy standing in for Othello.

(The actors are rehearsing IV-1. CHRIS plays CASSIO, DAVE plays IAGO, JIMMY plays OTHELLO with script in hand. The others are off book. In this scene, JIMMY is apart from the other two.)

CHRIS *(as CASSIO)*. I marry her? What, a customer? Prithee bear some charity to my wit! Do not think it so unwholesome. Ha, ha, ha!
JIMMY *(as OTHELLO)*. So, so, so, so. They laugh that wins.
DAVE *(as IAGO)*. Faith, the cry goes that you marry her.
CASSIO. Prithee say true!
IAGO. I am a very villain else.
OTHELLO. Have you scored me? Well.
CASSIO. This is the monkey's own giving out. She is persuaded I will marry her out of her own love and flattery, not out of my promise.
OTHELLO. Iago beckons me. Now he begins the story.
CASSIO. She was here even now. She haunts me in every place. I was the other day talking on the sea-bank with certain Venetians, and thither comes the bauble. By this hand, she falls thus about my neck!
OTHELLO. Crying, "O dear Cassio," as it were; his gesture imports it.
CASSIO. So hangs and lolls and weeps upon me, so shakes and pulls me. Ha, ha, ha!
OTHELLO. Now he tells how she plucked him to my chamber. —O, I see that nose of yours, but not that dog I shall throw it to.

CASSIO. Well I must leave her company.
IAGO. Before me! look where she comes.

(Enter LORRAINE as BIANCA.)

CASSIO. 'Tis such another fitchew! marry, a perfumed one! —What do you mean by this haunting of me?
LORRAINE as BIANCA. Let the devil and his dam haunt you! What did you mean by that same handkerchief you gave me even now? I was a fine fool to take it! I must take out the work? A likely piece of work, that you should find it in your chamber and know not who left it there! This is some minx's token, and I must take out the work! There, give it your hobbyhorse. Wheresoever you had it, I'll take out no work on 't.
CASSIO. How now, my sweet Bianca? How now? How now?
OTHELLO. By heaven, that should be my handkerchief!
BIANCA. If you'll come to supper tonight you may. If you will not, come when you are next prepared for. *(She exits).*
IAGO. After her, after her!
CASSIO. Faith, I must. She'll rail in the streets else.
IAGO. Will you sup there?
CASSIO. Faith, I intend so.
IAGO. Well, I may chance to see you, for I would very fain speak with you.
CASSIO. Prithee come. Will you?
IAGO. Go to: say no more. *(CHRIS exits as CASSIO but watches the scene.)*
OTHELLO *(coming forward)*. How shall I murder him, Iago?
IAGO. Did you perceive how he laughed at his vice?

OTHELLO. O Iago!

IAGO. And did you see the handkerchief?

OTHELLO. Was that mine?

IAGO. Yours, by this hand! And to see how he prizes the foolish woman your wife! She gave it him, and he hath giv'n it his whore.

OTHELLO. I would have him nine years a-killing! A fine woman, a fair woman, a sweet woman!

DAVE. Can we stop here?

CHRIS. Keep going.

DAVE. There's really no point without Othello. What are we supposed to be getting out of this?

CHRIS. I'd like you to layer the character more. Don't be quite so obvious.

DAVE. What I do depends on what Othello does.

JIMMY. I'm sorry, I thought I should act like I was hurt and...

DAVE. No, no, it's not your fault. You can't be expected to know what to do. You're not an actor, for heaven's sake.

CHRIS. All right, all right. Thanks, Jimmy. *(To LORRAINE and DAVE.)* I'll give you two notes, then I'll make calls. *(Giving notes.)* Dave, I want you more casual on "I am a very villain else."

DAVE. Casual?

CHRIS. You're still tipping your hand way too much. I want Iago much more subtle in here.

DAVE. I can't work up Othello if I'm so laid back.

CHRIS. Yes you can. It should look effortless. I need you in sync with the overall style of the play, Dave.

DAVE *(under his breath)*. And what style would that be?

CHRIS *(ignoring DAVE's comment)*. Lorraine, you're too laid back. I want you brassier.

LORRAINE. Brassier?

CHRIS. When you enter, you are furious with Cassio. Go at it. Even knock me around.

LORRAINE. She's not a ruffian.

DAVE. She's no Desdemona, either.

LORRAINE. Cassio says I am his wife.

DAVE. Cassio never says that. Iago says Cassio is "almost damned in a fair wife." Nowhere does it indicate that Cassio is actually married nor that Bianca is his wife.

LORRAINE. But she's not a whore.

CHRIS. Just do it brassier, Lorraine. Now do you have those phone numbers for me?

LORRAINE *(handing him pieces of paper)*. Shanks, Butler and Walker.

DAVE. Forget Billy Walker. He's Equity now.

CHRIS *(crumpling paper)*. Shit. Is Shanks any good?

GEORGIA. I don't think he's done any Shakespeare.

DAVE. That's all we need.

CHRIS. It doesn't matter at this point. I'm willing to train somebody.

JIMMY. Do you have notes for me?

CHRIS *(caught off guard)*. Uh, well...

JIMMY. So I can help Dave more.

CHRIS. Well, if you ask, I would be a little angrier here.

JIMMY. Okay, I thought he was kind of, you know, like in shock or something.

GEORGIA. Jimmy, would you let Chris make his calls, for heaven's sake?

JIMMY. Oh yeah, right.

CHRIS. So it's between Shanks and Butler. *(To LOR-RAINE.)* Wish me luck, babe. *(CHRIS goes to kiss LORRAINE. She stops him.)*

LORRAINE. Can we cut your line on my entrance?

DAVE. Here we go.

LORRAINE. Because Iago announces me and I want to come storming in on that. Can we cut the "fitchew" line?

DAVE. That sets up your entrance.

LORRAINE. I'm asking the director.

CHRIS *(harried)*. Leave it in, Lorraine. Look, people, run IV-3, Emilia/Desdemona, until I get back. Dave, watch it for me. Lorraine, would you schedule me tomorrow with Lodovico, Gratiano and the soldiers? *(Sighs deeply.)* Now let me go and find a damn Othello. *(Exits.)*

LORRAINE *(as stage manager)*. Set up for IV-3. *(She and GEORGIA begin to move flats.)*

DAVE. Blocking *Othello* without an Othello. Anybody else slightly worried about that?

GEORGIA *(with sarcasm)*. No, you'd be the only one, Dave. *(DAVE buries himself in his script. WENDY and JIMMY step aside to discuss the play.)*

WENDY. Take Chris' note. I think you needed to be a little more angry than surprised by the time you reached the end.

JIMMY. Are we doing that scene again?

WENDY. Not tonight. But that's okay. You and I can talk about where the real triggers for his anger come.

JIMMY. Okay.

GEORGIA *(moving flats, cubes, etc)*. Yoo-hoo, Miss Anne, I mean, Miss Desdemona. Could give us a hand with this stuff?

JIMMY. No, no, no. Let me take that, baby. You know you're not supposed to be doing that.

GEORGIA. Jimmy, I'm not an invalid.

JIMMY. None of you all need to be moving this. The three of you just sit over there. Dave and I can do it. Come on, Dave. *(DAVE joins JIMMY reluctantly, but they both set up while GEORGIA, WENDY, and LORRAINE move downstage, sip water, coffee, etc., out of JIMMY's hearing.)*

GEORGIA. Wendy, don't encourage him, please. I'm trying to get him to go home and you're giving him acting notes.

WENDY. Well, he's good, Georgia. Wasn't he terrific in that last scene?

LORRAINE. He's really into it, G.

WENDY. I think he's going to surprise the hell out of you one of these days.

GEORGIA. This is the one place I could come to get some space and now he's here. I can't have him all up in my business.

LORRAINE *(patting GEORGIA's tummy)*. Seems like he done *been* in your business, girl.

GEORGIA. You know what I mean. You'd think he was in the play. Every time I look up he's asking questions, shouting lines around the house.

WENDY. Maybe he really wants to act.

GEORGIA. Please!

WENDY. Would that be so awful?

GEORGIA. Yes!

JIMMY. Okay, you're all set up. You feeling okay, baby?

GEORGIA. I'm fine.

LORRAINE. Places for IV-3!

JIMMY. Am I in this scene?

GEORGIA. Man, go sit down!

WENDY *(aside to JIMMY)*. Watch this scene because it sets up Act V, Scene 2, "It is the cause my soul."

DAVE. Why are we doing this scene now?

WENDY. Just go with the flow, Dave.

DAVE. Very zen, Wendy. But this is no way to do Shakespeare. I'm sorry, but Chris has no experience at this.

LORRAINE. He's got fresh ideas. He's not weighted down with all those pseudo-English theatrical clichés.

DAVE. Like having an Othello?

LORRAINE. He'll find an Othello.

GEORGIA *(to DAVE)*. Just keep your mind on Iago.

LORRAINE *(to DAVE)*. And stay off Chris' back! IV-3 up please!

GEORGIA *(as EMILIA)*. How goes it now? He looks gentler than he did.

WENDY *(as DESDEMONA)*.
He says he will return incontinent,
And hath commanded me to go to bed,
And bade me to dismiss you.

EMILIA. Dismiss me?

DESDEMONA.
It was his bidding. Therefore, good Emilia,
Give me my nightly wearing, and adieu.
We must not now displease him.

EMILIA. I would you had never seen him.

DESDEMONA.
>So would not I. My love doth so approve him
>That even his stubbornness, his checks, his frowns—
>Prithee, unpin me—have grace and favor in them.

EMILIA. I have laid those sheets you bade me on the bed.

DESDEMONA.
>All's one. Good faith, how foolish are our minds!
>If I do die before thee, prithee, shroud me
>In one of those same sheets.

EMILIA. Come, come you talk!

DESDEMONA.
>My mother had a maid called Barbary.
>She was in love, and he she loved proved mad
>And did forsake her. She had a song of willow.
>And old thing 'twas, but it expressed her fortune,
>And she died singing it. That song tonight
>Will not go from my mind. I have much to do
>But to go hang my head all at one side
>And sing it like poor Barbary. Prithee, dispatch.

EMILIA. Shall I go fetch your nightgown?

DESDEMONA. No, unpin me here.
  (Singing.)
>   The poor soul sat sighing by a sycamore tree,
>   Sing all a green willow;
>   Her hand on her bosom, her head on her knee,
>   Sing willow, willow, willow

> The fresh streams ran by her and murmured her moans,
>> Sing willow, willow, willow;
> Her salt tears fell from her, and softened the stones—

Lay by these:—

> Sing willow, willow, willow;

Prithee, hie thee! He'll come anon.

> Sing all a green willow must be my garland;
> Let nobody blame him, his scorn I approve.

Nay, that's not next. Hark, who is 't that knocks?

EMILIA. It's the wind.

DESDEMONA.
> I call'd my love false love; but what said he then?
>> Sing willow, willow, willow;
> If I court more women, you'll couch with more men—

So get thee gone. Good night. Mine eyes do itch;
Doth that bode weeping?

EMILIA. 'Tis neither here nor there

DESDEMONA.
> I have heard it said so. O, these men, these men!
> Dost thou in conscience think—tell me, Emilia—
> That there be women do abuse their husbands
> In such gross kind?

EMILIA. There be some such, no question.

DESDEMONA. Wouldst thou do such a deed for all the world?

EMILIA. Why, would not you?

DESDEMONA. No, by this heavenly light!

EMILIA.
> Nor I neither, by this heavenly light.
> I might do 't as well i' th' dark.

DESDEMONA. Wouldst thou do such a deed for all the world?

EMILIA *(sitting next to DESDEMONA)*. The world's a huge thing. It is a great price for a small vice.

DAVE. Don't sit next to her! She's your mistress!

LORRAINE. That's how it was blocked.

DAVE. Emilia's the maid, so sitting down doesn't work. Georgia, you need to be more active here anyway.

WENDY. Chris wants it intimate. We're sharing dangerous ideas.

JIMMY *(from the sidelines)*. Yeah. Seems like you two are real tight.

DAVE. Thanks for the insight, Jimmy. Now, you stand behind her, Georgia, and brush her hair, starting with "'Tis neither here nor there."

GEORGIA. That's not what Chris wants.

DAVE. He asked me to look at it.

LORRAINE. Look at it, not rework it.

DAVE. Try brushing, Georgia.

GEORGIA. It's bad enough I'm playing a maid. I'm not doing that: "Oh mistress let this darky brush thy golden locks"

DAVE. Well you can't sit beside her.

LORRAINE. Leave it the way Chris had it.

DAVE *(throwing his script down)*. I'm going for coffee. Call me when you're serious.

WENDY. Dave, would you take it easy?

DAVE. Our star dumps us. We're stuck casting Othello two weeks into rehearsal. What little we've blocked, doesn't work. I told you this was a bad choice from the beginning. You all let political correctness, and commercial pressures dictate your artistic decisions and now we're in a bind.

WENDY. *Othello* is a great play and a great vehicle to attract our non-existent black audience.

DAVE. You find me a competent, non-equity, black actor who can pull off Othello in two and a half weeks and I'll dance naked in the aisle.

GEORGIA. In that case, please *don't* find anybody!

WENDY *(takes a risk)*. Well, I've been working on something that might be the solution to our problem.

GEORGIA. Tell me it's Dave in blackface!

DAVE *(sarcastically)*. Ha, ha.

WENDY. It's an incredibly simple solution.

JIMMY. Hold on, Wendy...

WENDY *(smiling at JIMMY, she continues)*. It happened by accident. I first thought he might understudy, but I think he's ready to...

(CHRIS enters from offstage.)

CHRIS. No luck. Butler was my last hope and he just took another job.

GEORGIA *(to CHRIS)*. Wendy says she's got somebody.

WENDY. Well, it's a possibility.

CHRIS. Who?

WENDY. He's never had formal acting training but he's talented. I've been working with him a lot and he's done well in just a short time. I know he could do it.

GEORGIA. So who is it?

WENDY. Jimmy.

GEORGIA. Jimmy who?

WENDY. Your Jimmy.

GEORGIA. Excuse me?

JIMMY. Me. *(A brief silence.)* That's how come I got dressed up. To audition.

GEORGIA. You're kidding.

WENDY. You've seen how good he is.

GEORGIA. As a blocking stand-in.

WENDY. We've gone over the script. He understands the language and action for each scene. We've even rehearsed the really tough ones...

GEORGIA. Rehearsed?

JIMMY. Wendy's been working with me since Jason left. I've been going to her school during my lunch hour and we worked here early sometimes.

GEORGIA. Are you out of your mind?

CHRIS. Can he do it?

WENDY. I think so.

JIMMY. I wanna try.

GEORGIA. Wait...wait a minute...

WENDY. Let him show you his audition.

CHRIS. You ready to audition? *(Pause. JIMMY checks GEORGIA's reaction. He hesitates when he sees her less than enthusiastic face.)*

GEORGIA. No, he is not. Jimmy, what are you doing?

JIMMY. Listen, G, I know you're surprised at all this. But from the first night when I saw Jason doing the part it was kind of interesting to me. I started reading the play a lot. One night, I was in the back messing around with lines and Wendy saw me.

WENDY. I happened to catch him at it. I knew Jason was shaky and I thought he'd make a good understudy. So I've been working with him.

JIMMY. First, I thought she was kidding. Even when I saw she was serious, I didn't know if I was going to do it. But then Lorraine asked me to do the blocking and I've been working almost every night so...

GEORGIA. As a stand-in.

WENDY. He's off book for quite a few scenes.

CHRIS. Well, I'll be damned.

GEORGIA. So those were your errands? You've been meeting her for lunch?

CHRIS. Can he pull this off?

WENDY. I think he can.

DAVE. You're suggesting that we cast a novice as Othello to open in two and a half weeks?

WENDY. He's good, Dave. He needs work, but he can do it.

JIMMY. If you don't think I'm any good, it's all right. I'll just sit my butt back down. But I can give it a shot.

GEORGIA *(to JIMMY)*. Why didn't you tell me?

JIMMY. I didn't want to tell you and then look like a jackass. I'm not as good as Jason.

WENDY. I think you're more natural. *(To CHRIS.)* We can show you V-2 Othello/Desdemona.

CHRIS. All right. Set it up. *(LORRAINE and WENDY begin to move flats and blocks.)*

DAVE. Are you serious about casting him as Othello?

CHRIS. If I like his work.

DAVE. The backbone of the play is the Othello/Iago relationship. Shouldn't we see if he's credible with me?

WENDY. We didn't work a lot with the Iago scenes.

DAVE. You have to at least see us together on stage. If those scenes don't work, we haven't got a play.

JIMMY. I've walked through some of those scenes.

DAVE *(as IAGO)*. Will you think so? *(Beat.)* Will you think so? Top of IV-1.

GEORGIA. I don't believe this.

WENDY *(hurriedly finding the scene in her script for JIMMY)*. We've only read through this a couple of times.

JIMMY. I remember it.

GEORGIA. I don't believe what I'm seeing here.

WENDY *(putting her arm around JIMMY to encourage him)*. Take your time, Jimmy? Remember to breathe at the line endings. You'll be fine.

(Beat. The scene begins. DAVE uses this opportunity to showcase his considerable acting skill. JIMMY is somewhat slow and uncertain, but that feeds directly into OTHELLO's disorientation and self-doubt in the scene.)

IAGO. Will you think so?
JIMMY *(as OTHELLO)*. Think so, Iago?
IAGO. What, to kiss in private?

OTHELLO. An unauthorized kiss!

IAGO.
> Or to be naked with her friend in bed
> An hour or more, not meaning any harm?

OTHELLO.
> Naked in bed, Iago, and not mean harm?
> It is hypocrisy against the devil!
> They that mean virtuosity, and yet do so,
> The devil their virtue tempts, and they tempt heaven.

IAGO.
> If they do nothing, 'tis a venial slip.
> But if I give my wife a handkerchief—

OTHELLO. What then?

IAGO.
> Why then, 'tis hers, my lord, and being hers,
> She may, I think, bestow 't on any man.

OTHELLO.
> She is protectress of her honor, too.
> May she give that?

IAGO.
> Her honor is an essence that's not seen;
> They have it very oft that have it not.
> But for the handkerchief—

OTHELLO.
> By heaven, I would most gladly have forgot it.
> Thou saidst—O, it comes o'er my memory
> As doth the raven o'er the infectious house,
> Boding to all—he had my handkerchief.

IAGO. Ay, what of that?
OTHELLO. That's not so good now.

IAGO.
> What if I had said I had seen him do you wrong?
> Or heard him say...

OTHELLO. Hath he said anything?

IAGO.
> He hath, my lord, but be you well assured,
> No more than he'll unswear.

OTHELLO. What hath he said?
IAGO. Faith, that he did— I know not what he did.
OTHELLO. What? What?
IAGO. Lie—
OTHELLO. With her?
IAGO. With her—on her—what you will.

OTHELLO. Lie with her? Lie on her? We say "lie on her" when they belie her. Lie with her—

JIMMY. What is this word again... "zounds"? *(He says it rhyming with "sounds.")*

WENDY. Zounds, it rhymes with "wounds." For "God's wounds."

CHRIS. Keep going! Move all over the place, Jimmy. Physicalize his agitation. Shout! Run up and down as much as you can, even with the script.

OTHELLO *(pacing back and forth)*. Zounds, that's fulsome! Handkerchief—confessions—

CHRIS. Don't be afraid to shout. Use the power of your voice.

WENDY. Big breaths.

OTHELLO. Zounds, that's fulsome! Handkerchief—confessions—handkerchief. To confess and be hanged for his labor. First to be hanged and then to confess—I tremble at it. Nature would not invest herself in such shadowing passion without some instruction. It is not words that shakes me thus. Pish? Noses, ears, and lips—is't possible? Confess—handkerchief—O devil! ...

(As himself.) You want me to fall down here?

CHRIS. No, that's fine, Jimmy. Just fine. *(WENDY hugs JIMMY. CHRIS and LORRAINE applaud. DAVE and GEORGIA are reserved.)*

JIMMY. I'm sorry. The end was bad. I never moved around when we did it before.

CHRIS. That's all right.

LORRAINE *(to JIMMY)*. You were good.

DAVE *(sighs)*. Boy, it would need an awful lot of work.

CHRIS. But he's got the heart of this guy. Wendy can coach him for the rest.

JIMMY *(looking at GEORGIA)*. What do you think, baby?

CHRIS *(pause)*. Georgia, what do you think?

GEORGIA. It doesn't matter.

JIMMY *(knowing GEORGIA is troubled)*. You don't want me to do it?

GEORGIA. It's just that... *(To the group.)* I need some time to talk to Jimmy. Can we take a break?

CHRIS. Let's break for fifteen.

LORRAINE *(announcing)*. I'm going to Chino's.

CHRIS. I'll come with you.

LORRAINE. Who wants what?

JIMMY. I'll take tea with lemon. *(Showing off for GEORGIA.)* Wendy says warm liquids are good for the vocal apparatus.

GEORGIA. Oh really. *(Calling to LORRAINE.)* Get me dark with extra sugar. *(To JIMMY.)* And don't say a thing to me about the baby!

DAVE *(exiting backstage)*. Get me a pint of gin and a good shrink!

WENDY *(following DAVE)*. The usual for me, thanks, Lorraine. Wait, Dave...

LORRAINE *(calling out)*. Be ready in fifteen, people! *(CHRIS and LORRAINE exit talking.)*

JIMMY. You surprised?

GEORGIA. What do you think?

JIMMY. I thought you would be happy.

GEORGIA. Jimmy, I'm glad you're interested in what I'm doing. Reading lines, standing in for blocking...

JIMMY *(enthusiastic)*. But like you said, it's kind of addictive. Once I started the blocking, I didn't even know what that was at first, but once I started moving around like him and all...

GEORGIA. That's just a walk-through, baby. Acting is *work*.

JIMMY. I think I can do it, G. Wendy's taught me a lot. If I can rehearse it for real...

GEORGIA. This is a major Shakespearean role! The language alone...

JIMMY. ...okay, the words are a little hard, but...

GEORGIA. A little hard? It's iambic pentameter!

JIMMY. But I know what he's saying, G. I know this guy. He's a brother, just like me. Wendy showed me the Larry Fishburne video and...

GEORGIA. For God's sake, Jimmy! Just because you're a brother and you saw a video, you think you can play Othello?

JIMMY. Okay. Forget it. You don't want me to do it. I won't do it.

GEORGIA. It's not that I don't want you to.

JIMMY. You don't think I can.

GEORGIA. It's just that...I...I...well, no I don't think you can.

JIMMY. Fine.

GEORGIA. Jimmy, I've got a master's in English. It took me years to do Shakespeare.

JIMMY. Oh, I see what you're saying. It took an educated person like you years to learn it. So a dumb nigger like me couldn't possibly...

GEORGIA. ...That's *not* what I'm saying!

JIMMY. Reaching down to the lower classes is fine, as long as you stay on top, huh, G?

GEORGIA. Damn it, Jimmy, that's my family's class hang-up, not mine.

JIMMY. I never did the whole degree thing, and that embarrasses you.

GEORGIA. It doesn't embarrass me and I'm telling you that has nothing to do with this!

JIMMY. Bullshit! See, I didn't want you messing around with this theatre crap from the beginning because I thought it would come between us. When I saw your Juliet, even with you slobbering all over the white boy, I said, "Okay, she says it's just a play. Be cool." So now the baby's coming. I ask you to stop. You say no, you just have to do *Othello*. I say, "All right, I'll hang out because I don't want you coming home on the bus by yourself all hours of the night. Maybe I'll learn something." I'm watching Jason and I'm thinking, "Hey, I *know* this guy." Wendy sees me messing around and offers to teach me. So, I'm thinking I'm going to surprise the hell out of you, right? Show you how smart I am. I'm working my ass off during lunch, late at night. *(He starts heading out through the house.)* But I'm just an asshole. The white woman tells me, "You can do this." My black woman tells me, "You can't do this. You're just a dumb-ass maintenance man."

GEORGIA. Damn it, Jimmy I'm *not* saying that!

JIMMY. Well maybe, you're right. If I'm still trying to prove myself to you, maybe we never belonged in the same place at all.

GEORGIA. That's not true.

JIMMY. I'm awake now.

*(As JIMMY leaves he bumps into CHRIS and LOR-
RAINE entering the theatre. They have no idea what has
just transpired.)*

LORRAINE *(announcing)*. Coffee's in the house!
CHRIS *(pulling JIMMY playfully by the arm)*. Tea with lemon for your vocal apparatus, sir.

(DAVE and WENDY enter.)

LORRAINE. Come get your stuff, guys. Georgia, here's dark extra sugar. Let's set up Jimmy in V-2, people!
JIMMY. Hey, Chris, I'm going to take off. I'm not doing this.
CHRIS. What do you mean?
JIMMY. I changed my mind. I don't have time to do this. *(Silence.)*
WENDY. What? Jimmy, come on.
JIMMY *(to GEORGIA)*. I'll pick you up later.
WENDY. Wait a minute. What happened?
LORRAINE. Talk to him, G.
CHRIS *(catching him)*. Jimmy, we're up shit's creek. We need you.
WENDY. You were just nervous because we haven't really worked the Iago scenes.
LORRAINE. Show us a scene with Desdemona.
WENDY. Let's do the murder scene. We've rehearsed that.
JIMMY. I can't. See, it would be all messed up now.
WENDY. No, it wouldn't, Jimmy, just use what you're feeling right now. Remember we talked about how Iago has Othello all messed up inside? I'll turn this around

for the bed. I'll lay here. *(She arranges some of the cubes.)*

CHRIS. You can use your script.

WENDY. He doesn't need it. Come on, Jimmy. *(Pause. JIMMY stands still, not knowing what to do.)*

JIMMY. Georgia doesn't want me to.

GEORGIA. No, go ahead. I want to see it.

WENDY. Come on, Jimmy. You've worked so hard. Let's show her. *(CHRIS puts his arm around JIMMY's shoulders and walks him towards the stage.)*

CHRIS. Look, Jimmy, Othello is scared. He's doubting everything he's ever known. The woman he loves has betrayed him, made him feel like a fool. Publicly humiliated him. He's got to end it. He's about to destroy the thing he loves most in the world.

WENDY. Pretend you have the candle, just the way we rehearsed it. *(Pause. JIMMY looks to GEORGIA.)*

GEORGIA. Go on. *(Pause. JIMMY begins almost inaudibly. He is unsteady, but has the power of a beginning actor who connects very deeply to the character he is playing. Everyone is still.)*

JIMMY *(as OTHELLO)*.

> It is the cause, it is the cause, my soul.
> Let me not name it to you, you chaste stars!
> It is the cause. Yet I'll not shed her blood,
> Nor scar that whiter skin of hers than snow
> And smooth as monumental alabaster.
> Yet she must die, else she'll betray more men.
> Put out the light and then put out the light.
> If I quench thee, thou flaming minister,
> I can again thy former light restore

CASTING OTHELLO

Should I repent me. But once put out thy light,
Thou cunning'st pattern of excelling nature,
I know not where is that Promethean heat
That can thy light relume. When I have plucked the rose,
I cannot give it vital growth again,
It needs must wither. I'll smell it on the tree.
O balmy breath, that dost almost persuade
Justice to break her sword!
(He kisses her and strokes her skin.)
One more, one more.
Be thus when thou art dead, and I will kill thee
And love thee after. One more, and this the last
(He kisses her and strokes her skin.)
So sweet was ne'er so fatal. I must weep,
But they are cruel tears. This sorrow's heavenly:
It strikes where it doth love. She wakes.

WENDY *(as DESDEMONA)*. Who's there? Othello?
OTHELLO. Ay Desdemona.
DESDEMONA. Will you come to bed, my lord?
OTHELLO. Have you prayed tonight, Desdemona?
DESDEMONA. Ay, my lord.

OTHELLO.
If you bethink yourself of any crime
Unreconciled as yet to heaven and grace,
Solicit for it straight.

DESDEMONA.
Alack my lord,
What may you mean by that?

OTHELLO.
>Well, do it, and be brief. I will walk by.
>I would not kill thy unprepared spirit.
>No. Heaven forfend! I would not kill thy soul.

DESDEMONA. Talk you of killing?
OTHELLO. Ay, I do.
DESDEMONA. Then heaven have mercy on me.
OTHELLO. Amen, with all my heart
DESDEMONA. If you say so, I hope you will not kill me.
OTHELLO. Hum!

DESDEMONA.
>And yet I fear you; for you are fatal then
>When your eyes roll so. Why I should fear I know not,
>Since guiltiness I know not, but yet I feel I fear.

OTHELLO. Think on thy sins.
DESDEMONA. They are loves I bear to you.
OTHELLO. Ay, and for that thou diest.

DESDEMONA.
>That death's unnatural that kills for loving
>Alas, why gnaw you so your nether lip?
>Some bloody passion shakes your very frame.
>These are portents, but yet I hope, I hope,
>They do not point on me.

OTHELLO. Peace and be still.
DESDEMONA. I will so. What's the matter?

OTHELLO.
> That handkerchief
> Which I so loved, and gave thee, thou gav'st to Cassio.

DESDEMONA.
> No, by my life and soul! Send for the man
> And ask him

OTHELLO.
> Sweet soul, take heed, take heed of perjury.
> Thou art on thy deathbed.

DESDEMONA. Ay, but not yet to die

OTHELLO.
> Yes, presently.
> Therefore confess thee freely of thy sin.
> For to deny each article with oath
> Cannot remove nor choke the strong conception
> That I do groan withal. Thou art to die.

DESDEMONA. Then Lord have mercy on me!
OTHELLO. I say amen.

DESDEMONA.
> And have you mercy, too. I never did
> Offend you in my life, never loved Cassio
> But with such general warranty of heaven
> As I might love. I never gave him token.

OTHELLO.
> By heaven, I saw my handkerchief in 's hand!

> O perjured woman, thou dost stone my heart
> And mak'st me call what I intend to do
> A murder, which I thought a sacrifice!
> I saw the handkerchief!

DESDEMONA.
> He found it, then.
> I never gave it him. Send for him hither.
> Let him confess a truth.

OTHELLO. He hath confessed.
DESDEMONA. What, my lord?
OTHELLO. That he hath used thee.
DESDEMONA. How? Unlawfully?
OTHELLO. Ay.
DESDEMONA. He will not say so.

OTHELLO.
> No. His mouth is stopped.
> Honest Iago hath ta'en order for 't.

DESDEMONA. O, my fear interprets! what, is he dead?
OTHELLO. Had all his hairs been lives, my great revenge had stomach for them all.
DESDEMONA. Alas, he is betrayed, and I undone! *(She weeps.)*
OTHELLO. Out, strumpet! Weep'st thou for him to my face?
DESDEMONA. O, banish me, my lord, but kill me not!
OTHELLO. Down, strumpet!
DESDEMONA. Kill me tomorrow, let me live tonight.
OTHELLO. Nay, if you strive—

DESDEMONA. But half an hour!

OTHELLO. Being done, there is no pause.

DESDEMONA. But while I say one prayer!

OTHELLO. It is too late. *(He smothers her. Pause. The room is still for a moment.)*

JIMMY *(turning to the group, simply)*. So that's it. *(LORRAINE, CHRIS, clap wholeheartedly. WENDY hugs and praises JIMMY. DAVE and GEORGIA applaud reservedly.)* It was better when we did it before. I was nervous.

WENDY. You've never had an audience before. You were terrific.

CHRIS. Jimmy, you were good!

JIMMY. What do you think, baby? *(Pause.)*

GEORGIA *(stonefaced, to JIMMY)*. You should do it.

CHRIS. So, we've cast Othello! *(WENDY, CHRIS and LORRAINE applaud and cheer and congratulate JIMMY.)*

JIMMY *(looking at GEORGIA)*. No. No. Wait, I don't think she wants me to. *(Pause. They all look at GEORGIA.)*

GEORGIA *(pause)*. It's fine.

JIMMY. No. I'm not going to do it.

GEORGIA. Do it.

CHRIS. Wendy will continue to coach you. We can start right now, from Othello's first entrance. We'll work through the whole play slowly to make sure Jimmy gets the blocking down...

JIMMY. I already know it.

DAVE *(interrupting)*. Wait a minute, wait a minute. Clearly Georgia is unhappy, and so am I. Can we talk about this? *(Pause.)* Jimmy, that was a good scene. I admire what you've done here, truly. But a scene isn't a play. Five minutes isn't twenty-five performances. Performing for us isn't the same as performing for an audience, not to mention screaming high school kids. And you need to think about a realistic level of commitment. Being a blocking stand-in isn't the same as performing a major role that carries an entire production. That's a lot of pressure and a lot of responsibility.

LORRAINE. Stop talking to him like he's a kid.

WENDY. Jimmy, I know you can do this.

JIMMY. It depends on what Georgia wants.

GEORGIA. No, it doesn't. You want to do it. So do it.

CHRIS. Georgia, do you have a problem with me casting Jimmy as Othello?

GEORGIA. Look, I have a problem with this whole damn play.

DAVE. You're not the only one.

LORRAINE. Shut up, Dave.

CHRIS. Children, please. Georgia, what's the problem? *(Pause.)*

GEORGIA *(as if a dam has burst)*. Desdemona loves Othello because he's the exotic black buck. Othello loves Desdemona because she's Miss Anne. Now I've got to play the maid to the alabaster goddess who Mandingo over here, played by my own *husband*, is drooling all over. Not to mention playing pregnant by my racist, slimeball husband Iago. I'm gonna tell you straight up, people, this is a struggle.

CHRIS. Georgia, first of all, you have to understand that *Othello* is a play about power.

GEORGIA. *Othello* is a play about race.

CHRIS. Power!

GEORGIA. Race!

LORRAINE. People, people, it's two mints in one, okay?

WENDY. Race is not everything.

GEORGIA & LORRAINE. Yes it is!

CHRIS. How can *you* think that?

LORRAINE. I'm black. Trust me on this one.

DAVE. This is exactly the reason why I opposed this play in our season. Once you start messing around with this kind of stuff...

GEORGIA. ...You discover what people *really* feel!

DAVE. ...You get into sensitive areas.

WENDY. Good! That's exactly what theatre is supposed to do.

DAVE. This racial stuff is always sensationalist. Face it, we're doing Jerry Springer with a touch of class.

CHRIS. I absolutely disagree. This is one of history's most beautifully written stories about human vulnerability...

WENDY. ...If New Vistas isn't willing to confront the issues, what the hell are we doing this for at all?

GEORGIA. Because we thought Jason's name would boost the bottom line. We wanted to get paid!

LORRAINE. And score points for the outreach grant.

CHRIS. Well, kids, for whatever reason, this is the play we're committed to. So how do we pull this off?

GEORGIA. By being honest.

JIMMY. I'd really like to play this guy.

GEORGIA. I don't want you playing a jerk.

JIMMY. He's not a jerk. He's very smart, he's just out of place.

GEORGIA. But the image we see is the big black buck lusting after the white woman.

WENDY. It's not because she's white. He's never had *any* woman pay attention to him.

JIMMY. His nose is so wide open, he doesn't know what he's doing. And this Iago dude has him all turned around.

WENDY. Othello's in love with love. It's got nothing to do with color.

GEORGIA. Oh, please! It's the same old stereotype.

DAVE *(half-joking)*. Maybe Georgia just doesn't want Jimmy playing love scenes with Wendy.

LORRAINE *(to DAVE)*. Maybe *you* don't want Jimmy playing loves scenes with Wendy. *(Noise as people speak over each other.)*

CHRIS. Wait a minute, wait a minute! Are we talking about the play now?

GEORGIA. I'm not going to lie. I'm not particularly thrilled about Jimmy rehearsing love scenes on a bed with a white woman.

JIMMY. What?

WENDY. You're kidding. *(Beat.)* Aren't you?

JIMMY. It's just a play. That's what you said when you did Juliet.

GEORGIA. Well, this is a very different play.

WENDY. I don't believe what I'm hearing.

GEORGIA. This whole play is about dishonesty. If we're going to pull it off, without killing each other, we have to be absolutely honest about how we feel.

WENDY. Then let me tell you that it honestly pisses me off when you call me "a white woman." We've been through too much shit together for you to reduce me to that.

GEORGIA. I'm telling you what I feel.

CASTING OTHELLO

DAVE. Since we're all being so brutally honest, may I just say...

LORRAINE. Here we go!

DAVE. To be blunt, I don't think Jimmy can play the lead.

LORRAINE. To be blunt, you want to play Othello.

DAVE. That doesn't even deserve a response.

LORRAINE. I used to watch you while Wendy and Jason worked. You had that same look on your face just now with Jimmy. You actually squirmed when he touched her.

DAVE. I squirm whenever I see bad blocking.

LORRAINE. Bullshit. It's his black hand on her white skin that makes you squirm. Why do you think *Othello* still packs the house after damn near four hundred years? You gave Desdemona and Othello the same look that Chris and I get on the street.

CHRIS. Anybody remember the word "acting"? This is just a play.

LORRAINE. There's no such thing, Chris, and you know it. It's your guts, your heart, and your ass on the line every time, or don't bother to show up.

CHRIS. It's a play about human vulnerability.

GEORGIA. Keep saying that enough and you might begin to believe it.

LORRAINE. It's about interracial sex.

DAVE. That's the problem! We need to shift the focus from sex back to Iago's malevolent manipulation...

GEORGIA. ...Shift the focus back to you...

LORRAINE. ...it's called *Othello*, not *Iago*...

JIMMY. Because he's the one who gets hurt the most.

DAVE. ...You're missing the whole point...

LORRAINE. *You're* missing the point, Dave. You always do. That's why your thing with Wendy messed up.

DAVE. What?

WENDY. Excuse me?

LORRAINE. Just because she's put you out of her bed, that doesn't mean it's over.

WENDY. Lorraine!

CHRIS. Let's keep it about the work, folks.

LORRAINE. You said you still have feelings for him. If he's overbearing, you just need to assert yourself more.

WENDY. Who died and made you Freud?!

LORRAINE. Hey, I tell the truth.

WENDY. With everybody else's business. Why don't you tell Chris the real reason you hate playing Bianca to his Cassio.

CHRIS. What's this now?

WENDY. She doesn't want to play your whore in front of your father.

LORRAINE. Bianca's not a whore.

CHRIS. We've been through this eighty times.

LORRAINE. You call me a monkey.

CHRIS. Cassio calls Bianca a monkey. He's just being defensive. He can't tell Iago how much he loves her.

LORRAINE. You call me a "fitchew." A fitchew is a prostitute and a skunk!

CHRIS. Do you think anyone is going to know what the hell a fitchew is?

LORRAINE. They'll know "monkey"?

CHRIS. So what?

LORRAINE. I'm a black woman, Chris.

CHRIS *(teasing)*. YOU ARE?! OH MY GOD!

GEORGIA *(a friendly warning to CHRIS)*. This is no time to be cute.

LORRAINE. Have you thought about what it means to have cast me in this role?

DAVE. It's a play!

LORRAINE. Which his father will see!

GEORGIA. Not to mention all the other white folks who think black women are nothing but monkeys, maids, or "fitchews," anyway.

DAVE. Oh come on.

GEORGIA. Wake up, Dave.

CHRIS. This isn't about race!

LORRAINE. Right. And neither are your screaming matches with your father.

CHRIS *(surprised)*. What?

LORRAINE. I've overheard your end of a couple of phone calls. I'm not stupid.

CHRIS. That's personal.

LORRAINE. So is the play!

GEORGIA. Our casting makes the racial stereotypes worse.

DAVE. Desdemona is white and Othello is black. Sorry, guys, we're stuck with what Shakespeare wrote.

CHRIS. Should I have cast Iago black?

LORRAINE. No! If Shakespeare had wanted Iago black he would have talked about his thick lips and sooty bosom too. Iago has to be white. That's why he takes Othello down. He's white and he can't stand to think of black Othello having more power than he does.

GEORGIA. Exactly. The way we're casting *Othello*, all the weak characters are black: Emilia the maid, Bianca the whore and Othello the fool, all duped by the powerful, white Iago. So when big black buck Othello smothers the hell out of fragile white Miss Anne Desdemona, what the hell do you think your audience is going to feel?

LORRAINE. The same thing Dave feels watching Wendy. The same thing your father feels watching us.

DAVE. All we've got is the text. Othello is a big tough guy who's just not very smart and he lets...

GEORGIA. That's the stereotype.

JIMMY. That's why I want to play him. He's not some big dumb black guy off the street. He's intelligent. He's sensitive inside.

GEORGIA. Chris, this is about more than us fractious little darkies making a fuss. We're all responsible for what's on stage. We have to be conscious of what we're doing and the message we're sending.

LORRAINE. That's why Georgia won't brush Desdemona's golden locks. That's why I won't wear that costume with my breasts sticking out. We're not going to reinforce those racist stereotypes.

CHRIS. I hate this obsession about race!

LORRAINE. You can hate it, but you can't deny it. The characters are obsessed by it, the audience is obsessed by it, and obviously, we are too.

GEORGIA. If we can't be honest with each other, we need to close it down.

CHRIS. Just walk away from it? Fine. Quit. Hey, that's the story of my life. Just as I get it together, everything around me falls apart. Well I've got too much at stake here. If I walk away from this, I know what I'll walk straight back into. Do you know what it takes for me to come in here night after night without an Othello? Dave looking over my shoulder, Georgia evil, Lorraine rewriting the script, me doubting my sanity. But I have to prove I can do this. To my father, to myself. Now, I'm doing the final roll call. I need to know who's in, who's out? You're free to walk. I'll recast your parts. No hard feelings. *(Pause.)*

WENDY. I'm in, Chris.

CHRIS. Thanks, Wendy. I need you. *(Pause.)* Casting Othello is the hardest part, Jimmy, I'm offering you the role with my ass on the line.

JIMMY. I want this, G.

GEORGIA. I don't want you out there like some wild black psychopath. All you need is a black scull cap and you're a wanted poster for the Aryan nations.

DAVE. What do you want to do, rewrite the ending? Othello and Desdemona go to marriage counseling?

GEORGIA. Of course not.

DAVE. Then what the hell are you talking about? *(Everyone argues loudly.)*

JIMMY *(whistles)*. Yo! Hey! Wait a minute, people. I think I see things a little different...

GEORGIA. Jimmy, please. You really don't understand...

JIMMY. Damn, Georgia! You keep telling me I don't understand. Why? Because I didn't go to college? But see, that's why I *do* understand. Othello's a soldier. A working guy like me. His home is the battlefield, right? But here he is living in the city. Just like my home is in the basement fixing stuff, but here I am hanging around a theatre with all you educated types, right? He's a working-class black dude, but here he is hooked up with a rich girl. Just like me, right?

GEORGIA. I ain't a white girl.

JIMMY. You were raised like one. Desdemona's father's having a shit fit because she married him. Hey, I know about that, right? And I bet Desdemona talked Othello into eloping too. *(He looks pointedly at GEORGIA.)*

GEORGIA. So what's your point?

JIMMY. Othello's around all these rich, educated folks, so he has to prove himself all the time—come off smarter, badder than everybody else. So when he thinks Desdemona played him he's really hurt, right? He thinks she just disrespects him and thinks he's stupid. She was the one person he needed to believe in him. He trusted her and she betrayed him. It's like treason to him, right? He kills her like a court martial, you know, like it's the honorable thing to do to a traitor on the battlefield. It's his idea of justice with honor. He's not a murderer in his heart.

CHRIS. Exactly.

GEORGIA. But you know every time people see a black man with a white woman he's got to be some kind of psycho-pimp.

JIMMY. But you can't play Othello like a pimp, because he doesn't know jack about women. The dude is clean, man. He's gentle. Desdemona is his first, right? That's why this hits him like a Mack truck.

CHRIS. I see what you're saying.

JIMMY. I don't see him like some wild man. I see him quiet. It's like when your own wife hits you in your weakest spot, ain't nothin' you can do, right? That's why it felt weird when you asked me to shout and run around and stuff. I thought he would be like almost crying, he feels so hurt.

CHRIS. It certainly shows a different side of Othello.

JIMMY. People wanna make brothers into monsters all the time. This guy's just a regular dude. I wanna show that.

Women cross the street away from me. Black women and white women. Like I'm going to hurt them. This guy didn't want to hurt nobody. That Iago dude just messed up his head.

CHRIS. All right, I'll buy that. So, will you do it?

JIMMY *(pause, then to GEORGIA)*. What did you think, baby? Am I any good.

GEORGIA *(pause)*. It was good.

JIMMY *(pause)*. So I can do it?

GEORGIA. Well, let's talk about renegotiating this maid thing too.

CHRIS. You're not a maid, you're...

GEORGIA. ..."just like a member of the family." Don't even!

CHRIS. I was going to say, you're Desdemona's confidant, her advisor, her friend.

GEORGIA. Well just don't make me brush her hair, and I'm in.

JIMMY. Oh, baby, I sure was hoping you'd say that. *(He hugs her.)*

GEORGIA *(pushing him away)*. Only because I don't want you coming home late on the bus by yourself.

CHRIS. All right then, it's Jimmy, Georgia, Wendy and me... *(A short silence.)*

LORRAINE. You'll have to recast Bianca.

CHRIS *(stung, but trying to maintain his composure)*. All right.

LORRAINE. I feel as if I'd be putting our relationship on stage.

CHRIS. I treat you like Cassio treats Bianca?!

LORRAINE. Hell no, because I'd never take that shit from you or anybody else.

GEORGIA. Speak!

LORRAINE. But I can't rewrite the part. I'd be living all your father's stereotypes of me on that stage.

CHRIS. So, you're leaving.

LORRAINE. The role, but I want to stay with you...as stage manager.

CHRIS. I see. *(Beat.)*

LORRAINE. And...you know.

CHRIS. What?

LORRAINE. I'm still your...friend...you know...

CHRIS. I believe the word you're choking on is "lover." *(He goes to hug her.)*

LORRAINE *(pushing him away)*. All right, all right.

CHRIS. You're a hard woman, Lorraine.

LORRAINE. I'll put out a call for a new Bianca. And she's gonna be ugly.

CHRIS. Dave, where do you stand? *(Beat. The cast looks to DAVE. He begins to pack up his stuff. The cast gets the message.)*

DAVE. Chris, I'm a founding member of New Vistas. I built our first set. I've acted in every production, and stage managed all but this one. Hell, I helped create the Board your father sits on. All I've ever wanted is to make what's on this stage the very best it could be.

CHRIS. I respect that.

DAVE. You know I wanted to direct the Shakespeare production this season.

WENDY. So did I.

CHRIS. And I appreciate...

DAVE. Wendy happily stepped aside to give you a shot. I stepped aside only because your father asked me to.

CHRIS *(heartsick)*. Oh, Dave. I never wanted that. I had no idea...
DAVE. I'm used to running things. Old habits die hard.
WENDY. We want you to stay, Dave.
DAVE. Do you?
WENDY. We all do.
DAVE. But, do *you*?
WENDY *(pause)*. Yes, I do.
DAVE. All right. So...I'll try not to be too much of a pain in the ass.
CHRIS. Dave, you'll always be a pain in the ass, but you'll also be a brilliant Iago. I'm really glad you're going to do it.
LORRAINE. Even I'm glad. How do you like that!
JIMMY *(teasing DAVE)*. Now I gotta kiss Wendy because that's what the script says. You're not going to kick my ass, are you?
DAVE. Well, I don't know about that.
LORRAINE. As if he could.
CHRIS. Lorraine and I will rework the schedule. We'll pick it up tomorrow night at six, people! *(Although all still feel the seriousness of the undertaking, there is an air of relief as they chat and prepare to leave. LORRAINE barks orders.)*
LORRAINE. Auditions for Bianca on Saturday. Call every ugly woman you know! Tomorrow night plan to work till midnight, at least. Dave, we'll want you and Jimmy for additional rehearsals, starting ten a.m. Sunday.
CHRIS. We'll start from the top tomorrow.
LORRAINE. I've got to call Brabantio, and Roderigo.
CHRIS. I'll come with you. Okay, people, I'm excited about this. See you all tomorrow night.

LORRAINE. Pick up your trash! Georgia come on and take Jimmy's measurements for me. I gotta phone them in to Theresa. *(JIMMY, GEORGIA, LORRAINE and CHRIS exit to the office.)*
DAVE. Thanks.
WENDY. You're a wonderful actor, Dave.
DAVE. But the rest of me is messed up.
WENDY. You just want too much too fast. Give it time.
DAVE. Is what Lorraine said true? Do you still have feelings for me?
WENDY. Lots. I just don't know what they are. *(Beat.)* Do you really squirm when Jimmy touches me?
DAVE. Yeah. But not because he's black. I don't like anyone touching you. *(Beat.)* I love you.
WENDY. I'm not ready to hear you say that yet.
DAVE. Then I won't. *(Beat.)* Can we have coffee?
WENDY. Okay.
DAVE. Tonight?
WENDY. Next week.
DAVE. My place?
WENDY. Chino's.
DAVE. That'll work.

(GEORGIA enters to get JIMMY's jacket.)

DAVE. Yeah, well, good night. *(He starts to exit.)*
WENDY. Can you give me a lift?
DAVE *(smiling)*. I'll wait outside. *(Exits.)*
GEORGIA *(teasing)*. You two leaving together, huh? *(WENDY does not reply.)* Is it back on? *(WENDY doesn't reply.)* You're mad about what I said?
WENDY. The "white woman" will be fine.

GEORGIA. You know how I meant that. *(Teasing.)* And you love this little evil pregnant black lady, don't you? You know you can't help it. *(WENDY is not amused. GEORGIA approaches her. She is sincere, although she tries to keep it light.)* I say what's on my mind and piss people off. *(Pause.)* Can you understand how I feel about the play?

WENDY. Of course. I can't understand how you feel about me coaching Jimmy. If you don't trust me with your husband what kind of friendship have we got?

GEORGIA *(serious, puts her arm around her)*. A good one. Because we don't bullshit each other. If we're really friends, I have to say what's on my mind. *(Pause. This is hard to say. She indicates her belly.)* I'm happy but I'm also feeling big and fat and ugly.

WENDY. But you're not.

GEORGIA *(indicating her belly)*. I'm wondering if this is right for me... whether I've made the right decision.

WENDY. You have.

GEORGIA. You had more confidence in Jimmy than I did.

WENDY. Because you didn't know what he could do. The important thing is that you're behind him now. He's going to need your support even more than mine.

GEORGIA. I appreciate what you did. *(GEORGIA hugs her.)* Only, I'll coach him from now on.

WENDY *(laughing)*. Yes ma'am.

DAVE *(calling from outside)*. You coming, Wendy?

GEORGIA *(teasing WENDY)*. You heard the man. Go on.

WENDY *(rushing out through the house)*. So I'll brush your hair in the scene. What do you think?

GEORGIA. I love it!

(WENDY exits as LORRAINE and CHRIS enter from backstage.)

LORRAINE. You two okay now?

GEORGIA. Yeah.

LORRAINE. Jimmy's trying on the shirt and vest. *(LORRAINE tosses GEORGIA her keys.)* Would you double lock when he's done?

GEORGIA. It's going to be good, Chris.

CHRIS. If you all don't kill me first. *(GEORGIA exits backstage.)* I want Jimmy rehearsing every chance we get.

LORRAINE. Larry needs to know about the program change and I have to get Jimmy's bio.

CHRIS. I was so scared that everyone would quit. *(Beat.)* Including you.

LORRAINE. Chris... if you're serious about... if we're really going to be...

CHRIS. "Lo-vers." *(Showing her how to say it.)* Put your tongue on your upper teeth—"lo-vers." Why can't we just relax and be in love? Why must every kiss become a major sociopolitical event?

LORRAINE. Don't you understand why I don't want you kissing me in front of people?

CHRIS. Lorraine, I'm sorry the world is so messed up. But I do love you and I'm going to want to touch you.

LORRAINE. What about what I want?

CHRIS. You want me. I want you. I will work as hard as I have to. I love you *because* of who you are, not in spite of it, you got that? And you love me because...? *(Beat.)* And you love me because...?

LORRAINE *(sarcastically)*. You're rich!

CHRIS *(seriously)*. I need reassurance too, Lorraine. I'm not the world's most confident recovering addict. Are we alone? Can I touch you now? *(He holds her.)*

LORRAINE. We're swinging without a safety net.

CHRIS. You talking about the play or us?

LORRAINE. Both.

CHRIS. I know we can do it, Lorraine.

LORRAINE. The play or us?

CHRIS. Both!

(They hold each other, looking into each other's eyes. After a beat, they hear JIMMY entering, running lines for GEORGIA. As soon as LORRAINE hears them, she moves away from CHRIS and gets busy again.)

JIMMY *(running lines as OTHELLO)*.
   ...Rude am I in my speech,
   And little blessed with the soft phrase of peace;
   For since these arms of mine had seven years' pride...

GEORGIA *(correcting sternly)*. Not "pride," it's "pith," "seven year's pith"!

LORRAINE. Lord, Jimmy, I pity you with a mean, old, evil teacher like that.

JIMMY. I know. Wendy never yelled.

GEORGIA. Get it right and I won't either! *(LORRAINE and CHRIS begin to exit through the house.)*

LORRAINE. Don't forget to double lock.

CHRIS. This is going to be *good*! *(They all say their good nights. CHRIS and LORRAINE exit. JIMMY continues gathering his things as he quietly rehearses his lines.)*

GEORGIA. I'll be patient.

JIMMY. No you won't. But that's okay.

GEORGIA. I'm ashamed.

JIMMY *(stung)*. Of me?

GEORGIA. No! No! I am proud of you. I'm ashamed of the way I...

JIMMY. What's the matter, baby? What's wrong?

GEORGIA. You don't have to prove yourself to me. I know you're smart.

JIMMY. I know you wish I had the education...

GEORGIA. I don't care about that.

JIMMY. Sometimes I think you only married me because of the baby.

GEORGIA. I married you because I love you.

JIMMY. I'd be watching Jason. I'd be saying, "I could play a general. I could do all that." I wanted you to be proud of me. I want your father to see me. I want to be able to say to our kid, "Kid, your old man played Shakespeare!"

GEORGIA. I was being selfish. I never thought about what you felt. I'm ashamed... *(She cries.)*

JIMMY *(strokes her hand)*. Come on, baby, it's all right.

GEORGIA. You kept saying you could do it but I didn't take you seriously. You shouldn't have had to go to Wendy. *I* should have taught you the part. *I* should have believed in you.

JIMMY. You did. You married me. You're having my child. *(Beat. Then playfully.)* You didn't think I could play Othello, but I faked you out. *(He sticks out his tongue.)*

GEORGIA. I am so proud of you. *(She hugs him.)*

JIMMY. See that. If Othello hadda hooked up with some Moorish sister in the first place, he wouldn't have gone through all them changes. Oh well, I got mine. *(They kiss.)*

BLACKOUT